INVENTOR ANONYMOUS

The shocking true story behind the world's biggest patent monopoly, the Automobile Title

Kathleen Keith

Copyright © 2019/2020 by Kathleen Keith.
All rights reserved

No part of this publication may be reproduced, stored in a retrieval system, or transmitted in any form, or by any means, electronic, mechanical, photocopying, recording or otherwise, without written permission from the publisher, except for the inclusion or brief quotations in a review.

For information about this title, or to order this book contact the publisher:
Kathleen Keith
kkeithauthor@gmail.com
Website address: www.inventoranonymous.com

Book illustration header by Joe Doll
Book cover image created by Alex Winter
Cover design by Ajibola Alabi

978-1-7344983-0-1 Paperback
978-1-7344983-1-8 Hardcover
978-1-7344983-2-5 E-book

Contents

Dedication 5
Disclaimer 6
Acknowledgments 7
Introduction 8
Chapter 1   The Beginning of the End 11
Chapter 2   In Remembering 17
Chapter 3   Way Back When 21
Chapter 4   Venturing Out 24
Chapter 5   Hopes and Expectations 28
Chapter 6   The Story Unfolds 61
Chapter 7   The Acorn Sprouts from the Mighty Oak 66
Chapter 8   Lakeshore Drive 70
Chapter 9   A Twinkle-Toed Kindergartner 84
Chapter 10 Knock, Knock. Who Might This Be? 88
Chapter 11 The Cold Reality Sets In 94
Chapter 12 The World Keeps Turning 102
Chapter 13 Moving On 109
Chapter 14 I Owe I Owe. It's Off to Court We Go 114
Chapter 15 Lightning Can Strike Twice 120
Chapter 16 Reprieve Awaits 124
Chapter 17 The Journey Back 142
Chapter 18 On The Road Again 156
Chapter 19 The Keysers 160
Chapter 20 Father's Coming 177
Chapter 21 Lessons Run Amok 195
Chapter 22 The Return 201

Chapter 23 Separation 206
Chapter 24 Cold Water Flats..218
Chapter 25 A State Of Constant Flux....................................225
Chapter 26 Juvi Nightmare 230
Chapter 27 Convent 245
Chapter 28 The Exodus... 251
Chapter 29 Final Thoughts 258
Chapter 30 Kathleen's Reflections..265
About the Author.. 268

Dedication

This book is dedicated in memory of my mother, Eleanor Snyder Leffew, whose story becomes the foundation of concern for all creative people. This true story is told through the eyes of Eleanor. She was Cecil L. Snyder's oldest daughter, and she wished to dedicate her life story to all of Cecil's descendants. Under God's watchful eye, and with His guiding hand and His inspiration, her story now comes forward. Eleanor's commitment to Jesus Christ was steadfast her whole life. She wanted to be counted with the sheep not the goats, as do I.

Disclaimer

This true story is based on my mother's recollections. To the best of her knowledge and memory, these are her truths and opinions.

Acknowledgments

I would like to acknowledge with gratitude the following individuals: Lisa Palmisano, a truly dear friend, whose skill and expertise is incredible and very much appreciated. You are amazing. Alyce Stelzner, my dear and wonderful friend, who has always been there for me at any given notice, I sincerely appreciated all the time you spent helping me move this story forward. Thank you both, so very much. I also wish to thank Steven Snyder, the catalyst, who emphasized the importance of family ancestry. To my cousins, Leo, whose phone call started me on this journey; Chrissy, who provided me with the courage, strength and very generous financial support to continue with this venture; Arthur, and his daughter, Kelly, who both were incredibly supportive and extremely generous; my brother, Billy, who is very dear to me; my good friend, Suzanne Arias, who is truly awesome; thank you all for being there for me. A very special thank you is in order to the incredible staff at Poplar Creek Library, for I greatly valued their technical assistance. Thank you, Brian, Alex, Colin, Brandon, and Rosha. And finally, a sincere appreciation goes out to all those who helped bring this truth to the surface.

Introduction

The time for honesty is at hand, for there is an undeniable hunger for truth and desire for transparency from governmental bodies. People need to know about injustices. This story is about Cecil L. Snyder and his massive monopoly, the Automobile Title Registration. His patented and copyrighted idea was infringed upon by the government and finally usurped, causing severe hardship on his entire family.

This story will reveal the problem with Sovereign Entity infringement and the impact it has on inventors and their families. **Inventor beware**, *it is legal*. You see, theft of intellectual property has always been a concern to the inventor who can seek out justice through the judicial system when infringement occurs, but when the government infringes on the inventor there is no place to turn for that justice.

This is why I must declare that all inventors have their rights restored to them as granted by the Constitution of the United States and the just laws of our land of this great country of America. Yes, the patent monopoly does carry connotations of unfounded fear, and for too long this fear has weakened the protection afforded by the judicial system against infringement of patent rights. The government should honor the inventor's patent rights; their ideas and creative thoughts belong to them. No inventor should feel the dread of having their patented idea taken away from them, just because their idea becomes huge.

This story is about the Automobile Title Registration, which was considered the biggest patent monopoly in the world, how it came to be invented and how this invention fell into the hands of the government. It is a story about my mother's family, my grandfather, and what the State Department did with regards to the grave injustices they inflicted upon their entire family in order to usurp the patent and copyright of the Automobile Title Registration, for the "good of the people," as they so boldly put it.

This story is the complete behind-the-curtain look at the life of Cecil L. Snyder, who is the inventor, author, and patentee of the Automobile Title Registration. He was president of his own corporation, The Automobile Abstract & Title Company of Detroit, Michigan and Chicago, Illinois. He was a man, a husband, a father and a grandfather who cherished principles above expediency and money. His personal dedication to receive just compensation for the infringement and the usurping of his patent by the government was pursued through the same legal system granted in the Constitution. Throughout this story and his many struggles with the governmental bodies, he remained dedicated in this pursuit.

In relationship to the facts in this story, one cannot explain away everything that happened in my grandfather's life as a giant mound of circumstances or just plain bad luck or coincidence. On the other hand, one will not be able to overlook the fact that what happened with regard to this story was most unusual, if not extraordinary.

My mother had one purpose in mind: She wanted to vindicate her father's image and release a true and valid picture of a man born into this world, a sheer genius in his own right, an uncommon man and quite probably the last of his kind.

INTRODUCTION

Come; ready yourself comfortably in a nice sofa or chair, in preparation for a wild ride into the land of truth, as my mother, Eleanor, tells her story. Many men boast of a dream that never came true, but few men tell a tale of a wild ride into their own nightmare. This grim, grimy tale quite possibly could scare the pants off you, for grandfather's story was a living purgatory. This is no fairytale. It is historically true.

CHAPTER 1

The Beginning of the End

This is Eleanor's story, in her own words.

In the winter of 1963, which was the coldest ever recorded in fifty-one years in Illinois, many people were sick with the flu and just the task of keeping warm was burdensome. I had been corresponding with my father quite regularly. I had just received his letter, dated January 31, 1963, saying he was ill. However, he felt that he was getting better and it was nothing serious.

The following month, on February 14, a bitter cold Valentine's Day, the silence in our home was shattered by the ringing of the phone as we were just about to sit down to our evening meal. It was the Wheaton police informing us that on February 13, a Mr. Cecil L. Snyder had passed away in Washington, D.C.

As I hung up the phone, feeling the full impact of what this message revealed, I became overwhelmed with emotion and began to weep aloud. I could not and would not let myself believe the truth of the matter. My heart was pounding as I gasped for breath. Thoughts of confusion ran through my mind. It had been only a few days prior that I had received his letter. An icy sensation of shock flowed through my body and chilled my very bones. In my haste, I had forgotten to ask the officer for complete information before I hung up. My husband, Bill, assured me that my patience would be rewarded with another call, possibly the next day, and he was right.

Eleanor and Bill

The following evening, another call came from the local police. It was the same message, only this time it was coming from the Homicide Division, in Washington, D.C. Spectacles of horror raced through my mind. *Homicide! What?* This word spelled out sinister connotations, and my blood boiled with beads of sweat breaking through my pore barrier, as preconceived thoughts emerged.

Then I received another call from a woman who identified herself as Father's landlady. She informed me that the Washington District of Columbia, Department of Welfare Office of Investigation and Collection had tried to contact me. I was utterly confused. Grief and mixed emotions overpowered my rational thinking, making it difficult for me to communicate.

I needed to gather my family together for consultation and discussion about our current miseries. Our friends and other informed people warned us that we should not risk becoming involved with the Department of Investigation and Collection Department. They thought that involvement could ultimately lead to an expensive funeral cost. My children were very young, and our family funds were undeniably meager to say the least. We could not raise enough money to go around the block, let alone Washington, D.C. There was absolutely nothing any of us could possibly do to either have my father's body returned to Illinois or become involved with exorbitant burial expenses in a far-off city. Father lay dead in a cold morgue waiting for someone to claim his body. With the family thousands of miles away, we were unable to reach out and claim him. We were victims of circumstances beyond our control.

Then the phone rang again. This time it was a man who refused to give his name. He said he was a friend of Father's and promised that he would give Father a decent burial with the help of Father's landlady. Both he and the landlady were surely grieved as to Father's plight and told me that unless I granted permission and contacted the Public Welfare and Collection Department, they could do nothing. The poor man was most insistent in his pleading. He warned that if I did not respond, Father would be cremated or his body possibly salvaged for a medical school cadaver. This stranger felt my father deserved a decent departure, but his plea fell upon my unwilling deaf ears. Our hands were tied by the simple fact that we did not have the money and could not allow our already heavily mortgaged home to go under jeopardy or be assessed.

My baby sister, Juanita, volunteered to go to Washington if we could finance the trip, but we were hopelessly bankrupt of funds. Juanita, who was a waitress in a big motel, could get the time off, but since she was making very little income and had three children with a house to maintain, she could not manage the financial burden either. So, we sent a letter to the morgue in Washington, D.C. relating our plight.

The landlady had informed me that Father had no personal belongings, only a small radio and a beat up old cane used for the blind, along with several boxes of Matzo crackers. She remarked, "Oh yes, your father had some personal mail, but all these things were confiscated by the police along with the radio and cane." She thought that my letters were probably in the bunch. I couldn't help but smile through my tears thinking of Father and his Matzo crackers. He had spoken of buying ten boxes in one of his letters.

When the police report came through, it stated death was caused from a heart attack and dehydration. Father, who claimed never to have been ill a day in his life, refused a doctor's attention during his last hours. The landlady quoted his last words, "Please go away and let me die in peace."

In reflecting back, I actually believe he may have anticipated his own death weeks before and was reluctant to worry me. I had been typing some business papers for him that he had requested prior to January of that year. Illegible scribbling of an almost blind person was the prelude of an obvious revelation that his life would soon reach a climax.

In the weeks before his death, he sent through the mail a rather shabby-looking package containing what looked to be the emptying of his bureau drawers. Among the rubber bands, balls of string, copper wire, paperclips, and childhood mementos were his badly stained patents and copyrights, as well as his patent book, dating back to the early 1900s, and a few Matzo crumbs thrown in for good measure. Also contained in his belongings was a booklet of Christian origin. This booklet caught my eye. I had been corresponding with Father in the hopes of being assured that he had received the message of Jesus Christ. This was important to me, and I wanted it to be important to him as well.

Turns out, in his last letter he had asked me to keep his patents and copyrights for future reference and had sadly remarked, "Maybe someday this government will have a change of heart." On this sad note, it was days later that his eyes were closed in death. As a tired voyager, he passed receiving no pardon for living or being born. I beg the government's pardon, for I hope they will excuse any dust particles he left lying around which might jog their memory. Never would he pound pavement again in his search for help. He nobly withstood the onslaught of almost fifty years of persecution and battling the government. Yet, never once did he waiver. He continued to his dying day to seek justice from the government and their infringements on his patent and copyright.

There was no beating of any drums heralding his passing. No parades, only lonely silence and the possibility of cadaverous embalming with formaldehyde or the smell of a burning cremation to acknowledge his memorial.

As Shakespeare once said, "What's in a name?" I'll tell you, Cecil L. Snyder, that's who. He was a man that no one knew, a man with no grave marker and no acknowledgment of his gifts to mankind. He gave of himself in a loving manner while being in the state of bankruptcy and blindness, as he related to everyday living in anticipation of his next invention.

CHAPTER 2

In Remembering

Several years before my father's death, we had informed him in our letters of his visible presence being sorely missed in our family circle. Also, the grandchildren were complete strangers to him and had far too long been deprived of his administrative and paternal observations. He was unwilling to allow us to administer to his needs of old age. He did not want any pity. Somehow, we were unable to get our message across because he resisted, wishing to not burden his children or the grandchildren. We even went so far as to suggest that we should try to borrow some money for a trip to see him, which was just prior to his death, but the very mention of our coming upset him. He seemed to want to discourage us from doing so, making statements that the area where he lived wasn't safe, and the expense for us would be great. He cautioned us to reconsider such a trip. However, he did express gratitude regarding my letters and told me it brought him great cheer.

With only the exchange of letters, he spoke of his love for his wife Minnie, my mother, and all of us, his children. He also shared the difficulties he was having with the Welfare Department hampering him from receiving an old-age pension. He indicated a lady representative of the District Department of Washington was threatening to send him a copy of the law because he had challenged her about him receiving his small entitled pension.

My oldest son, Billy, who was serving in the Navy on a ship called the *Ranger*, positioned off the shores of Vietnam, would also write to his grandfather. Billy sent Father a picture of the ship he was stationed on, but Father noted in a following letter that although he had received the picture, he could not see it well enough to enjoy it. Father's condition was probably due to cataracts which his famous home remedies could not cure.

In our written communications, I could clearly see that Father was still showing signs of enthusiasm believing that someday he would reach the Supreme Court to get what was rightfully his, but instead he died in utter poverty. Time would reveal that his confidence would slowly dry up and his long-carried burden would slip from his shoulders only when the hands of death reached out to greet him.

After my father's death, we had his patent carefully investigated by reputable lawyers who felt that this was a one-of-a-kind story. To their knowledge, there were no other cases with any similarities existing in history. They believed that according to law, as it stands, it would be impossible for this to ever happen again. These lawyers found my father's patent to be perfectly valid and remarked that there was certainly nothing wrong with the legality of it.

They researched and found that never in history had one man ever received a patent for anything similar, nor was there any case where the patentee was suing twenty-eight or more states, and the federal government for patent infringement. No other case was on record, for the states had infringed in this manner. Even though my father had gone the proper routes to fight this legally in court, with many lawyers, they were stopped at every turn.

The lawyers tried to explain Sovereign Immunity to me. They told me that states are Sovereign Entities. They have sovereign immunity under the 11th Amendment, and are immune from being sued in federal court, unless the state has waived immunity by an express statement or action. In other words, a state can steal your intellectual property and you cannot sue them for infringement, not unless they give you permission to do so. *Yes, this is legal.*

My father, who had taken every measure available through the legal system, did not prevail. Father went bankrupt fighting for his rights in the courts. The same courts who refused to hear the case because they would not recognize him with their permission.

I was told that if I could come up with the money, these lawyers just might be able to bring a suit in the courts, making an appeal to the legislature for back royalties on the infringement under the 14th Amendment, which allows for compensation. They thought there might be a slim possibility but cautioned that we could lose this time as well, relating to us that we hardly had a leg to stand on since the statutes had all expired. But in order to get the ball rolling, we would have to pay out thousands of dollars for legal fees and old court transcripts, which were buried in the court warehouses in Detroit, Michigan.

We were warned that it would be an uphill battle. In fact, the lawyer went even further and cited a case from back in 1903 titled, Standard Fireproofing Co. v. Toole et. al., 122 F. 649. The plaintiff had sued several officials of the State of Montana for patent infringement. I quote part of the court's decision as follows: "The patented partitions described in the bill are in possession of the State Government of Montana. It is using and enjoying the same. While it may not be in the power of the complainant to sue the state government, it may appeal to that state government through the legislature, for proper relief, but in my judgment should not seek to make the members of the state board or commission individually responsible for damages when it appears they have committed no wrong."

Et tu, Brute? Need any more be said?

CHAPTER 3

Way Back When

With ancestry being an important part of people's lives, Cecil's ancestry was traced back to the early 1600s. Back then, the city of Philadelphia, Pennsylvania, with its liberal government and its policies of religious tolerance, was becoming a refuge for many European immigrants, especially persecuted seculars. No other place was so concentrated representing so many different races and religions. The population then was mostly German and Dutch, whose language was High German. The descendants of these people today speak a corrupt German dialect largely known as Pennsylvania Dutch.

Among the German settlers were the family known as Hoch. They were very well-to-do farmers. The Hoch families of Middleburg, Pennsylvania, were the direct descendants of the German Dutch immigrants. John Hoch married a woman named Elizabeth Swainford. They had one daughter, Mary Magdalena Hoch, born in the year 1846. She married Edwin Samuel Long.

Their marriage produced only one daughter, Imogene May Long, born in August 1869, in Philadelphia, Pennsylvania.

Imogene May Long was an elegant lady of delicate taste and manners. She was highly educated, groomed and polished with culture. She spoke High German in the home. She was also a graduate of the Philadelphia Conservatory of Music and played the piano.

She married Henry Elmer Snyder in 1891, after he finished ministry school. Henry and his wife, Imogene, providing the necessities in life, shared their family residence with her widowed mother, Mary Magdalena Hoch Long. Their marriage produced three sons, John David, the youngest; Alpha Nicholas, the middle boy; and Cecil Le Roy, the oldest, born on March 24, 1892.

Their three boys, Cecil, Alpha and John, were healthy, happy boys nurtured in cultured refinement and mutual respect. Daily endeavors included all the normal humdrum chores which make up the rule of family life before the 1900s. Sunday was a day of worship, family gatherings and sharing of religious expression, which was the mandate for a father who was a minister of the church.

Cecil, being the oldest, was pampered not pushed. His father would many times brag or boast about his son. He would say with pride, "Imogene, that son of ours has a real head on his shoulders; he's going to go places someday."

With his parents at the helm, together they guided Cecil's probing and examining. He was an analyzer. He fostered extraordinary skill with his excellent refined penmanship, mathematical wizardry and detailed drawing capabilities of an engineer. He was a mighty fine doodler of design and was unknowingly preparing for stardom.

Cecil's abilities would move him toward the tide of life with refreshing vigor, but little did he realize an unforeseeable circumstance would pull his family apart like strings of taffy, tearing apart their family togetherness.

His traditional family life became shattered when his father, Henry Elmer, separated from his mother. This separation caused his mother and his grandmother to be forced to depend on their own resources.

There was little time now for quilting at the church, and daydreaming was out of the question for these good ladies. This new situation left them in dire need. Their overwhelming priority became survival. Fortunately, Cecil was ready to take over where his father left off. He was aspiring for the almighty monetary status, and his loved ones prayed for his achievements. Time was ticking toward future destinations.

CHAPTER 4

Venturing Out

In 1908, as our country was growing at a very slow pace, Cecil, who was tall, lean and lanky, a mere 16 years old, had a showcase of talent at his fingertips. Setting out as a nomad, he said farewell to his younger brothers, Alpha and John, and his mother and his grandmother, leaving behind his family in the fragrant farm hills of Pennsylvania.

Turning to look back only once to view his rural home site and his family stationed on the steps, he waved goodbye and wiped a manly tear from his eye. There was a job to be done and he was the chosen one. Grandmother shed a tiny tear as her grandson's figure faded from the focus of her eyes. She knew full well the task at hand was not going to be an easy one. "He's so young," she sighed. In her thoughts, she realized that a whole lifetime might have gone in another direction had their family not suffered this separation.

Circumstances were such that Cecil set his course by the compass of fate. He was destined for the big metropolis of Detroit, Michigan, drawn magically toward the Great Lakes region.

With the security of his mother's lunch, which she thoughtfully packed, fully tucked up under his arm, Cecil accomplished the first miles with his arms swinging and his legs flying, pacing himself with steady determination.

After lunch was finished and the brown paper bag lay crumbled along the roadside, all contacts with home ties were completely severed. He was no longer a boy, for he had taken on a man-sized job.

A good number of days passed, and his pace gradually slowed as he trudged from one road to another, one town after another, slowly fading into the sunset. Tediously he proceeded toward his destination. He was not one to shirk his duty to his family, for his two younger brothers looked up to him for their deliverance from their circumstances.

Traveling was not easily accomplished in 1908. This inexperienced lad found that he had to stop many times along the dusty path to rest his tired, aching feet or quench his frequent parching thirst, or even obtain directions. Thumbing a ride was not new, but the opportunities for this type of travel were lessened by the odds against any traffic going any great distance. Modes of travel were by cumbersome carriages and bulky buckboards, or even horseback.

With his sights focused on Detroit, he was thinking jobs were plentiful there. The carriage building business was booming. Henry Ford, Sr. had established a strong automobile business. Many were migrating to Detroit with one purpose in mind, and that was gainful employment. Henry Ford was building his cars, and the world soon began to roll right along. The cry was, "Better get a horse!" but nobody was listening as the horse and buggy fell by the wayside, disappearing into the annals of time with the rest of the old ways.

Strangely enough, Cecil did not seek employment at the Ford plant. Instead he sought employment with Maxwell Motors. Cecil's employment there was a run-of-the-mill job assisting the paymaster. During his employment at this establishment, he became good friends with Eddie Rickenbacker, who raced for Maxwell Motors.

After establishing himself securely at steady work, Cecil began to save his money for the day of promise when he could bring his brothers to Detroit from the Pennsylvania rural existence. His refugee-type living arrangement was extremely modest, to say the least, but sufficient. When the time was right, Cecil wrote home to Pennsylvania and sent a request for his brothers, Alpha and John, to join him in sharing his humble living quarters. Alpha joined forces with Cecil, putting their noses to the proverbial grindstone. Before long, they had enough money saved to begin house hunting on their own.

Cecil's mother patiently remained in Pennsylvania until she could sell the home and settle the family affairs. Her two older boys were already getting future plans into progress for the long-awaited family reunion. With diligence on their part, the boys located a proper potential investment. It was a neat bungalow with a bit of surrounding property. It seemed well-suited for a family of three grown boys, their mother and their grandmother.

Cecil Snyder (left) Alpha Snyder (right) John David Snyder (seated)

CHAPTER 5

Hopes and Expectations

Highland Park was the location of this desired property. It provided a tranquil setting of trees and flowers reminiscent of the past with its something old, something new environment. It captured the essence of days gone by, a paradise with a German flavor.

The moving process has always been full of stress. The brisk business of loading and unloading furniture from the boxes and unpacking the family treasures was a time-consuming and tiring chore. However, the housekeeping procedures went swiftly with plenty of able bodies to assist. Soon, everyone was comfortably settled into the confines of their new home. It was then they rested and gave thanks for their reunited family circle. It was indeed a time of new beginnings.

Six years whirled by, and with the three Snyder boys all gainfully employed at the Maxwell Motors plant, everything seemed to be fine. The year 1914 rolled around with rumors of war. It caused the people to begin to worry and to fret. In June of that year, Europe burst into war after the assassination of the Archduke Franz Ferdinand.

Alpha and John were drafted, but they were unable to pass the physical. Cecil could not pass either because he had a herniated groin, a condition he had since before age ten. Undaunted by their first experience and combined failure to be admitted to the fighting forces, they turned their talents to the essential work of their employer, Maxwell Motors.

In the fall of 1918, when the end of the war was in sight, the nations of Europe were exhausted and all concerned were determined to prevent a new war from breaking out.

On the home front, there were emerging dilemmas. The profitability of stealing a car in those days was growing by leaps and bounds, so much so that it was keeping pace with the development of the auto industry.

Stealing cars was a good way to make a living without working. Occasionally an automobile thief was sent to prison, but this percentage was small. The carelessness of auto owners was a constant invitation to new recruits to enter the thievery business. Countless mechanical devices were on the market, but the clever automobile thief was still able to apply his trade of profitability in comparative safety. In those days a man was never sure of the ownership of his car except when he was in possession of it. Once the car was stolen, chances were it was gone for good.

It was true that mechanical devices were the best safeguards against automobile theft in the U.S.A. at that time, but they were not 100% effective. So, Cecil, between the age of sixteen and twenty-four, began working on designing, developing and composing a method of making it impossible for the thief to dispose of a stolen car. His idea was a vehicle registration protocol that would establish a link between a vehicle and the vehicle owner. This would act as a crime deterrent. He patented and copyrighted his idea along with establishing a business called the Automobile Abstract & Title Company.

His company advertised this concept in an editorial from the *Chicago Tribune*, dated May 21, 1919, as part of the Automobile Abstract pamphlet, titled Registration for Automobiles, and reads as follows:

> *"Automobile stealing has grown to such an extent that it seems almost to have attained the respectability of sound commerce. Dozens of cars are stolen each week. The traffic increases in volume. Few punishments result. The burden falls on the unfortunate victims of theft. Ownership of an automobile has become a hazard.*
>
> *One of the immediate effects of wholesale thievery is an advance in insurance rates to an almost prohibitive point. To the original cost of a car must be added almost ten percent for insurance and a variety of locks. The car is stolen, the insurance company pays - and up go the rates again.*
>
> *The ease with which cars are stolen, shipped to other cities, or dismantled and disposed of piece-meal has invited the participation of many persons who might otherwise devote themselves to nobler pursuits.*
>
> *An occasional insurance agent may discover profit in conspiring toward the disappearance of a car. And, even policyholders have been found not incapable of lending themselves to fraud.*
>
> *We believe it would be to the advantage of the automobile organizations to seek legislation making the registration*

of automobiles compulsory in the sense of real estate. It should be required of an owner disposing of a car to show good title and pass that title legally registering the transaction. Possession without title should be prima facie evidence of fraud or theft.

The sale of an automobile nowadays is of no more moment than the sale of a bag of peanuts. It is not attended by any more restrictions. The result is the promiscuous hocking of cars. We urge some stringent method of controlling the traffic."

Cecil had perfected a system to effectively stop for all time the established business of stealing automobiles. The method he devised made it *impossible* for the thief to dispose of a stolen car.

Between the years 1909 and 1916, Cecil L. Snyder worked out his method and then applied for the copyright on December 17, 1917. The United States issued his copyright registration, axxc491, 492.

On May 7, 1919, Cecil filed for the patent, Abstract of Title and Method of Making the Same, serial No. 295, 297. The United States Patent Office issued patent number 1,433,975 on October 31, 1922, to Cecil L. Snyder of Detroit, Michigan. In good faith, he had staked his claim with the government.

Patented Oct. 31, 1922.   1,433,975

UNITED STATES PATENT OFFICE.

CECIL L. SNYDER, OF DETROIT, MICHIGAN.

ABSTRACT OF TITLE AND METHOD OF MAKING THE SAME.

Application filed May 7, 1919. Serial No. 295,297.

To all whom it may concern:

Be it known that I, CECIL L. SNYDER, a citizen of the United States of America, residing at Detroit, in the county of Wayne and State of Michigan, have invented certain new and useful Improvements in Abstract of Titles and Methods of Making the Same, of which the following is a specification, reference being had therein to the accompanying drawings.

My invention aims to provide a structural abstract of title and a method of carrying the abstract into effect so that it becomes a constant and positive weapon against theft, misconveyance, and surreptitious use of property, particularly an automobile or similar vehicle.

Briefly described, an automobile abstract of title is in the form of a book adapted to be issued to the owner of an automobile and used for the life of the car. The book includes a constructive arrangement of forms, some of which are in duplicate, and the most important of which is the bill of sale. Upon the purchase of a new automobile from the manufacturer's distributer, or upon the purchase of a used or secondhand automobile from an owner the bill of sale is made out by a notary public and sworn to. A duplicate of the bill of sale is also prepared by the notary and forwarded to the party issuing the abstract of title book. Triplicates of such bill of sale may be forwarded to the Secretary of State, State motor vehicle department, police department, or any places where a record of an automobile may be advantageously maintained.

Besides the bill of sale or certificate of ownership, there are special forms for additional sales or transactions and a similar record is adapted to be maintained so that throughout the life of an automobile there will be a complete history or summary arranged in chronological order, showing the origin, title, encumbrances, liens and liabilities to which an automobile may be subjected. Further carrying this into effect, there are pages in the book providing forms, records of any mortgage, contract or lien instrument, and other pages are devoted to forms constituting notices and the recording of any mortgage, contract or lien instrument. With such a structural arrangement of forms and by carrying out a method in accordance with my invention, it is possible to guarantee and prove the title of an automobile upon demand; to prevent any one selling or purchasing a stolen automobile; to afford protection and assist in obtaining loans and loaning money on automobiles; to prevent many court suits that otherwise follows sales transactions; to aid insurance companies and prevent an automobile thief or dishonest abstract holder from making fraudulent claims; to reduce theft hazards for insurance companies and consequently reduce insurance rates, and, to aid and assist State license bureaus and police departments.

My invention and the method of carrying it into effect will be hereinafter more fully considered, and reference will now be had to the drawings, wherein

Figure 1 is a plan view of one of the pages of a book form embodying features of my invention;

Fig. 2 is a similar view of the reverse face of the page;

Fig. 3 is a similar view of another page of the book form, and

Fig. 4 is a similar view of still another page that may be included in the book form.

The book form, mentioned in the beginning, comprises a suitable cover or folder in which the leaves or pages may be suitably bound, it being preferable to bind the upper ends of the leaves or pages in the upper folded portion of the cover so that the book is somewhat of manuscript form capable of being folded in a documentary manner.

The first page in the book form, as illustrated in Fig. 1, is adapted to have its upper end or edge 1 held by staples, stitchings or other binding means, and the right hand edge of the page is formed integral with a duplicate page 2 adapted to be folded on the weakened or perforated tearing line 3 into parallel registration with the bound end of the page. Page 2 is practically a duplicate of the bound in page and considering the main page, which is a permanent record for the owner of an automobile, the page is divided into three portions 4, 5 and 6 by transverse lines, and these same transverse lines are carried onto page 2 as perforated lines so that portions of the duplicate page 2 may be separated and used for specific purposes, as will hereinafter appear.

Patented Oct.31, 1922

Patent, page two

It started with the boy from Pennsylvania who had a dream that his idea would grow. With the help of a pencil, he sketched with an architect's skill and slowly his method emerged to take shape into the finished product. A new business was born, created and shaped by the same Cecil L. Snyder, inventor, author and patentee of the Automobile Abstract, who now would become the president of his own company, The Automobile Abstract & Title Company, incorporated April 18, 1918, forming a covenant and declaration of trust dated January 20, 1921.

A new way to stake a claim has not been found as of yet. This was the right and reasonable way to progress a patent and copyright.

The Abstract Plan consisted of a book form issued to the owner for the life of the car. There was provided in the abstract a bill of sale in consecutive order and attached to each bill of sale, a duplicate in the same consecutive manner. Upon purchase of a new automobile from the manufacturer, distributor, or upon the purchase of a used or second-hand automobile from an owner, the bill of sale would be made out by a notary public and sworn to before him. The notary would then detach the duplicate bill of sale and mail same to the office. Then the Automobile Abstract & Title Company would mail to the purchaser of the automobile his guarantee of title which was to be attached to the abstract by the purchaser. The transfer fee for each and every transfer was not to exceed two dollars and fifty cents. From this amount the notary would deduct their fee and the rest went to the Automobile Abstract & Title Company. The abstract system was to apply to all makes and types of automobiles.

THIS COVENANT AND DECLARATION OF TRUST, made this twentieth day of January, A. D. 1921, by and between

       Cecil L. Snyder, of Detroit, Michigan
       Michael Brogre, of "   "
       Albert F. Webb, of Franklin, Indiana
       Homer J. Richer, of Chicago, Illinois

herein designated "Beneficiaries" for themselves and their assigns; and

       Cecil L. Snyder, of Detroit, Michigan
       I. M. Snyder, "   "   "

together with their successors, herein designated "Trustees", WITNESSETH:

  WHEREAS, it is proposed by the Trustees to acquire from the Beneficiaries, certain cash, securities and property, as shown in a Schedule identified by the signatures of the parties hereto and filed with the Trustees; and

  WHEREAS, it is proposed that the property from time to time held by the Trustees and the business conducted by them, shall be divided into shares of beneficial interest, to be evidenced by certificates, as hereinafter provided; and

  WHEREAS, the purpose of this instrument is to create and provide for the administration of a TRUST, the parties to which shall be the Trustees and the several and unassociated Beneficiaries, and the subject of which shall be the TRUST ESTATE.

  a— The expression "Trust" as hereinafter used, signifies all of the Trustees, whether original or successors, qualified and acting at the particular time, regardless of their number. The expression "Trust Estate" as hereinafter used, signifies all of the property of whatsoever kind held by the trustees as such at the particular time. The expression "Beneficiaries" as hereinafter used, signifies the owners and holders of shares of beneficial interest in the Trust Estate at the particular time.

  NOW, THEREFORE, the Trustees do hereby acknowledge receipt by them of all cash, securities and property detailed in the aforementioned Schedule, and do hereby declare that the cash, securities and property hereby conveyed to them, and all other cash, securities and other property hereafter acquired by them as such Trustees, together with the proceeds, incomes, profits, increases and surplus thereof, shall be and become and constitute a Trust Estate, to be held, controlled, managed and disposed of by the Trustees for the benefit of the holders from time to time of the shares of beneficial interest in the Trust Estate, in accordance with the agreements and covenants herein set forth; to-wit:

ARTICLE I.

  FIRST: The trade name of this Trust Estate shall be AUTOMOBILE ABSTRACT AND TITLE COMPANY, and it may deal and be dealt with either by said trade name or in the name of its trustees. Its principal office shall be at Chicago, Illinois.

  a— Normally the trustees shall be two in number, and these declarants shall be the original Board of Trustees. Their number may be increased at any annual meeting, or regular or special meeting of the trustees, called for that purpose, and the trust shall vest in the additional trustees in connection with those already in office, the same as if they were original parties to this instrument.

  b— Each trustee shall hold office during the term of trust, or until their successors have been appointed and accepted this trust. A trusteeship may become vacant by death, resignation or removal.

Declaration of Trust Document

HOPES AND EXPECTATIONS

Abstract Plan Booklet

The prospectus for the Automobile Abstract & Title Company was printed and the advertising was launched in the *Motor News*, March 1919.

Motor News - March - 1919 - Volume 1 # 9

Stop the Automobile Thief!

DEMAND AN ABSTRACT

HAVE YOUR CAR PROTECTED

☛ Make application now. Blanks furnished upon request.

The abstract is fully protected by the United States copyright and patent laws.

There is just one way to effectively stop for all time the established business of stealing automobiles: *Make it impossible for the thief to dispose of the stolen car!* A thief steals to sell a car—not to use it for his pleasure. Deprive him of a market and you reduce theft. This is the idea and plan conceived by the Automobile Abstract & Title Company. The sale of an automobile often involves as much money as a sale of real estate. The abstract of title is always an important consideration in the transfer of real estate. Why shouldn't it be just as important in the transfer of an automobile? Land abstracts give the history of titles to property and its location. Automobile abstracts will give the history of titles to the automobile and its description. The abstract system will make it impossible to disfigure the car, alter and change the original car numbers without detection, and this, you know, is now being done every day in the disposing of stolen automobiles. Certain precautions have been taken in perfecting our system so that it is absolutely impossible for the thief to forge an abstract or evade the provisions of our plan in any way.

Facts
- It is a guarantee and proof of title with the automobile and upon demand.
- It will prevent anyone from selling or purchasing a stolen car.
- It will be a protection and important in obtaining loans and loaning money on automobiles.
- It will prevent many court suits that do otherwise follow sales transactions and it will be eventually demanded in and by the courts.
- It will be an aid to the insurance companies and prevent the automobile thief or dishonest policyholder from making fraudulent claims.
- It will reduce the theft hazard for the insurance companies, thus reducing insurance rates.
- It will be an aid to the State's license bureaus.
- It will be an aid to the Police departments.

Automobile Abstract of Title

Plan— Under our plan the Abstract will be issued in book form to the owner and used for the life of the car. There is provided in the Abstract bills of sale in consecutive order and attached to each bill of sale is a duplicate in the same consecutive manner. Upon the purchase of a new automobile from the manufacturer's distributor or upon the purchase of used or second-hand automobile from an owner the bill of sale will be made out by a notary public and sworn to before him. The Notary will then detach the duplicate bill of sale and mail same to our office. We will then forward this duplicate bill of sale to the Secretary of State. We will then mail to the purchaser of the automobile his guarantee of title which is to be attached to the Abstract by the purchaser. The transfer fee for each and every transfer shall not exceed two dollars; of this amount the Notary shall deduct his fee, which shall not exceed fifty cents, and mail to us the difference. The abstract system will apply to all makes and types of motor vehicles.

Automobile Abstract & Title Company

Executive Offices: BOOK BUILDING, DETROIT, MICHIGAN

Phone: Cherry 3360

Stop the Automobile Thief flyer

HOPES AND EXPECTATIONS

> To those who read me
>
> My name is prospectus. It cost money to print me. I was printed for a purpose and good cause. When you have read me through give me to your fellow friend. I intend to earn the cost of my printing and of coming to you for your information and benefit.
>
> I hope that I have conveyed to you the first step towards your success and prosperity. I am good for a limit of time. I must work fast.
>
> I trust you will not destroy me, but pass me along.
>
> Very Truly yours,
> Prospectus

The Prospectus

AUTOMOBILE ABSTRACT AND TITLE CO.

Executive and General Offices
Chicago, Ill.

ORGANIZED UNDER THE COMMON LAW

A DECLARATION OF TRUST

PROSPECTUS

Organization and Financing

"The ability to discern an opportunity in advance of the crowd is rare —so rare that the possession of this faculty means the great difference between wealth and poverty."

Prospectus, page two

Abstract Number   Application Number

APPLICATION for
Automobile Abstract of Title

Applicant's Name..Address...
                                                                                             Number   Street
Town or City..County of................................State of.................................
Trade Name....................................Year Made............Type of Body........................Model..................
Motor Number...Serial or Car Number...
Number of Cylinders..............................Manufactured by...
Date of Purchase..Did You Buy it New or Second Hand?....................
Purchase Price ($................................) Is it Insured?...............If so, by Whom?.................................
Are You Buying it on Contract?...................If so, State Whether or Not a Conditional Contract..........
Is it Mortgaged?..If so, to Whom?..
Amount of Mortgage..........................($..................) Date Mortgage Was Recorded.......................
Where Recorded?...............................
Are You a Dealer in Automobiles?..............................Are You a Manufacturer's Agent?...................
If so, of Whom?.................................
Are You a Licensed Agent or Dealer?..............................
Vendor's Name..Address...
                                                                                      Number   Street
Town or City................................County of......................State of...
Is Vendor a Dealer in Automobiles?....................Is Vendor a Manufacturer's Agent?.......................
If so, of Whom?...Is Vendor a Licensed Agent or Dealer?...................
1918 License Number...................................Issued by State of...
1919 License Number...................................Issued by State of...

NOTICE—The Notary is requested to see that all spaces in the above application are properly filled in, and that his seal is affixed in space allotted for the same.

                                                                                                                                                Applicant's Signature

State of..
                                    } ss.   NOTICE—Applicant should demand receipt of Two Dollars and Fifty
County of...   Cents ($2.50) upon payment to agent

On this..day of..................................A. D. 19......personally appeared before me...
who being first sworn, deposes and says that.............................the applicant named in the above mentioned
                                                 (insert he is or is agent for)
application and that he has signed the same and that the matters therein stated are true to the best of his knowledge and belief.

Notary's Impression Seal   Notary Public in and for said County and State
                                                                         My Commission Expires................................A. D. 19......

Received of...19......

Two Dollars and Fifty Cents ($2.50) as payment for application of an Abstract of Title with abstract service on a...automobile, motor No..................
owned by..., Address...
                                                   AUTOMOBILE ABSTRACT & TITLE CO.
....(Seal)   Per...(Seal)
                Underwriters   Solicitors
                EXECUTIVE OFFICES: BOOK BUILDING, DETROIT, MICHIGAN.

Automobile Abstract Title

Automobile Abstracts of Title <u>will</u>

Reduce theft insurance rates at least 50%.

Stop the sale of stolen automobiles.

Destroy forever the market for stolen automobiles.

Prevent dishonest persons who purchase stolen cars from obtaining licenses.

That it will abolish fradulent bills of sale and fake notary publics.

That it will be accepted in all courts of law as proof of ownership.

That it will enable a car owner to borrow money on his car and still retain possession of it.

That it will provide the only possible record of a motor car from factory to scrap-heap.

That it will show all replacements of parts and will record all vital repairs.

That its features for recording mortgages, liens, etc., will provide much needed protection for buyers of second-hand cars.

That its protective features will promptly reveal the whereabouts of stolen cars regardless of location or forms of concealment such as defacing car or motor numbers.

That it will prove of vast assistance to police departments and state license bureaus and will result in the saving of many hundred thousands of dollars to municipality and state.

That it will eliminate any possibility of switching auto licenses from one car to another thus giving the state department a check on each car and result in greatly increased revenues.

That it will not only add to the efficiency of the motor vehicle department but will reduce overhead 90%.

That its universal use in every state in the Union, Canada and Mexico, and other Foreign Countries, will standardize the transfer of motor cars.

That it not only protects a car but also assumes full liability by guaranteeing the motorist's title TO THE FULL EXTENT OF THE PURCHASE PRICE.

Believing that the automobile abstract of title is a much needed reform in the present indiscriminate manner of handling motor car transfer, I hereby pledge myself not to purchase, in future, any automobile to which clear title cannot be shown by an automobile abstract of title.

Signed ....

Underwriter and Special Agent

....(Seal)

| Number | Street | | Town or City |

INSTRUCTIONS

Read the application over very carefully before filling in. Be sure your motor numbers are correct. Having properly filled out the application, do not erase, alter or scratch out any statement or answer made therein, or in any manner deface same. A Notary Public with seal, or Justice of the Peace must fill out the affidavit.

The affidavit fee including services rendered in connection with obtaining this application, by the Agent, Notary Public or Justice of the Peace, shall not exceed One Dollar ($1.00) which amount shall be deducted from the application fee of Two Dollars and Fifty Cents ($2.50).

Promptly upon receipt of this application and One Dollar and Fifty Cents ($1.50), which amount covers all expense of services in recording this application, the Automobile Abstract & Title Company will furnish an abstract free of charge.

All payments to this office must be made in certified checks or money orders.

All money sent by mail will be at the risk of the sender.

If any of the above instructions are not complied with, the application will not be honored by this office.

WRITE LEGIBLY AND IN INK

AUTOMOBILE ABSTRACT & TITLE COMPANY, Detroit and Chicago

Automobile Abstract of Title will

Cecil's established business, the Automobile Abstract & Title Company, had both executive offices and general offices established in Detroit and Chicago. The offices in Detroit were first located in the Ford Building, and then later they were expanded to the Book Building. In Chicago, several floors of offices were rented in the Palmolive Building.

Cecil had big plans for his business future. He then went on to design drawings for what was to be the *tallest office building in the world*. He envisioned a building all made of colored glass, with five to nine basements. The location was to be Chicago, Illinois. He designed this building by himself and patented and copyrighted his idea, patent pending 1926. Signatures of people interested were autographed on the original specifications for this building.

The area of North Michigan was the chosen site for this massive building. Quite incidentally, this is the same area where the John Hancock building now stands, recognized as the tallest building in the world, outside of New York City, back in the 1960s. This John Hancock Center was created by an architect by the name of Bruce Graham. Cecil L. Snyder designed one identically the same height *some forty-two years prior*. Did they wait until Cecil was dead and gone before erecting this memorable ghost in the purple fringes of the horizon? I wonder and ponder the coincidences.

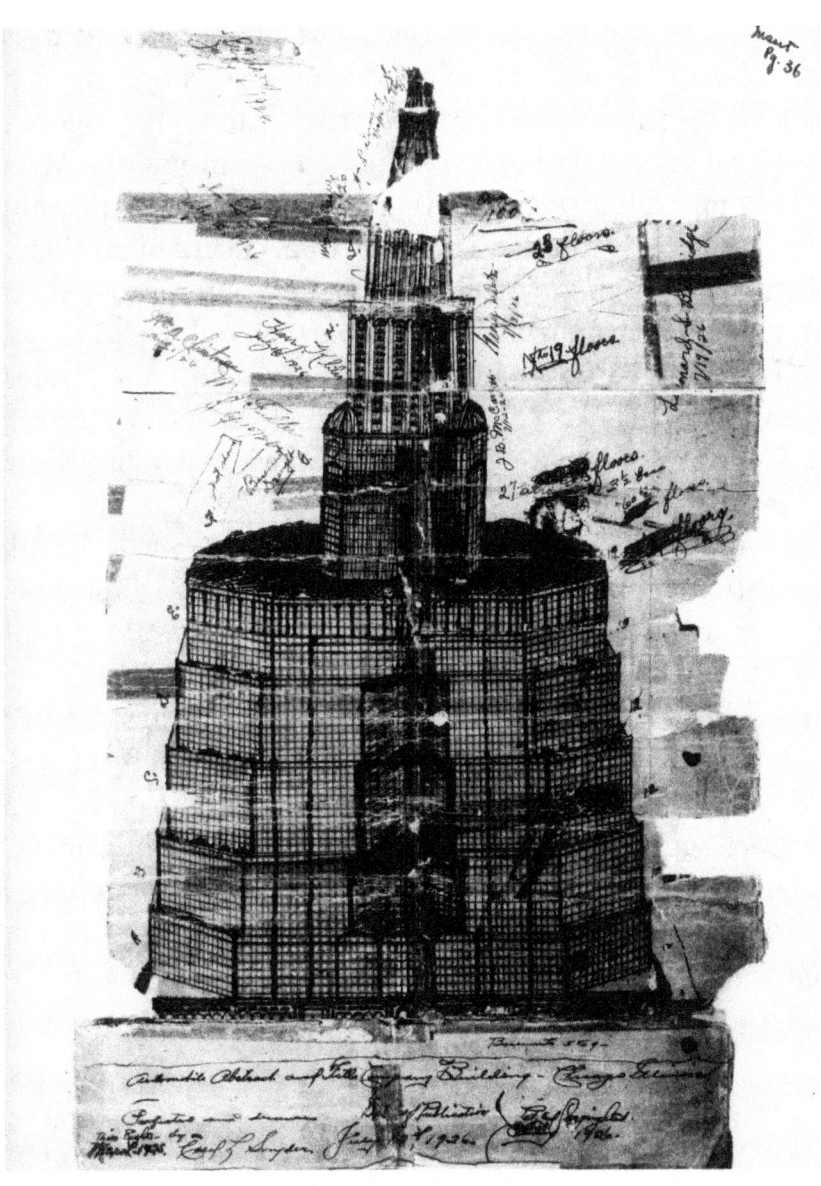

Original building drawing with signatures, designed for The Automobile Abstract & Title Company

Cecil loved the city of Chicago, but his hopes and dreams were crushed because the rulers of America were against him. The government did not want one man to have a business that would turn out to be a huge monopoly. The Automobile Abstract &Title Company had estimated earnings of twenty to fifty million dollars annually, after deducting the total cost of operations.

As a businessman, Cecil held many conferences with the leading insurance men and automobile clubs all over the county. This resulted in the heartiest endorsement of the preferred system that Cecil L. Snyder invented. Even Henry Ford, Sr. approached Cecil and was interested and wanted to buy the idea, but Cecil wasn't interested in selling.

The Automobile Abstract & Title Company was a Michigan Corporation capitalized at one million dollars. At first they did not offer any stock for sale, although they expected to place upon the market their treasury stock, which was to sell at par value of ten dollars. Seven men were the organizers, officers and directors of the company. Later, many men left their other positions and companies or jobs and joined in the new business that Cecil generated. They got on board. With excitement and anticipation, they acted with monumental action and performance. It was considered to be the biggest, best thing to come along in business history.

Sample stock specimen

National Underwriters, July 17, 1919, wrote an article titled, "Plan of Automobile Abstract & Title Explained by Cecil L. Snyder, President of Company, Offering New Idea Tells of Niche It Is Expected to Fill." In this article, Cecil Snyder, the company's president and inventor of the abstract system, made a statement. The statement reads as follows:

> "At the present time there are in excess of 6,000 motorcars in general use. Theft rates have reached an altitude where they are rapidly getting out of reach for the average man. Only 40% of all cars carry theft insurance and that percentage will continue to decrease in exact proportions

as rates go up. New cars are coming from the factories at a rate of 7,000 per day with the promise of 10,000 per day the following September. These are interesting figures, but they become more than interesting when considered in connection with theft losses. They become vital, all important. The automobile abstract is going to solve this problem. It is going to bring down theft rates very materially and by so doing, it will most certainly greatly increase the volume of policies now written. It is going to eliminate theft by the simple process of making it impossible to sell a stolen car. Insurance companies will benefit with the motorists' lower rates, a bigger volume, minus losses. It is an ideal condition and possible only by the abstract of title. Its beneficial effects will be reflected in all other classifications too, for it will allow the motorist of modest means a chance to invest in collision, liability and property damage if he so desires."

It was thoroughly investigated and carefully prepared. Intensive study and testing was applied for three years. All angles were questioned as to its relationship to manufacturer, distributor and insurance underwriter.

There was an air of breathlessness about the whole operation. Everyone everywhere wanted to get in on the ground floor. Cecil's mother and brothers, John and Alpha, put together their life savings and invested in Cecil's business. The family remained cool as all seemed to be in good favor.

At the tender age of twenty-seven, Cecil L. Snyder, author, inventor, and patentee of the Automobile Abstract, was the president of his own company. Cecil wanted to share his good fortune with everyone. The Automobile Abstract & Title Company was destined to be a worthwhile and lucrative business.

The Automobile Abstract & Title Company was an expressed trust, titled: "Organized under the Common Law, a Declaration of Trust." This trust was divided into Common Shares and Preferred Shares.

A sum exceeding two hundred thousand dollars had been spent to thoroughly test the business functions of this company. The business was endorsed by everyone, and thousands of people were hired to work. Advertising was given to the Club Magazine. In fact, this would be the very first advertising listing given them from the Abstract & Title Company. Two hundred and fifty thousand dollars was spent on this venture. An advertising manager was hired. Even Eddie Rickenbacker was almost coaxed into joining his good friend's business, but other things kept him preoccupied. However, he did give Cecil a great endorsement. I quote it. "It is the most important step that has been taken to prevent theft and to bring the legitimate exchange of ownership of automobiles to a standard that will protect all concerned."

With millions of dollars at stake, it was "the biggest thought in motorcar protection since the advent of the automobile itself..." quote from *Chicago American* newspaper.

Millions of Dollars at Stake, pamphlet

Contained inside the Automobile Abstract & Title Company's pamphlet, "Millions of Dollars at Stake," the *Chicago Tribune, the Chicago Evening Post, Pittsburgh Dispatch, Detroit Journal, New York American, Detroit Free Press, St. Louis Globe Democrat, Milwaukee Sentinel, Minneapolis Tribune, Insurance Field, US Review, Washington DC Herald*, the police departments and the motor clubs, all fully endorsed and sponsored The Automobile Abstract & Title Company.

James Couzens, a multi-millionaire, summed it up by saying in a statement to the *Detroit News*, that he gave them credit that by having a complete monopoly, which they had, that they should show earnings of $1 million and furthered his statement, "For the business done in the State of Michigan only, a better endorsement, upon its merits, we could not wish for."

Even John D. Rockefeller quoted, "Don't delay; get it while you can." Was it possible Rockefeller was prognosticating a warning based on his own experiences with the government with his monopoly, the Standard Oil Company?

Yes, Cecil L. Snyder had a complete patent monopoly with an absolute sole exclusive right to practice the protected invention. The Automobile Abstract & Title Company, a continuous business organized under the safe and most sound method, should have been protected by the Constitution of the United States. It was to be designed, controlled and managed under the ruling of the courts of equality, all drafted by experienced engineers. With shareholders from coast to coast, Canada and other countries, it was endorsed by everyone and, best of all, it would reduce crime with car theft.

Automobile Abstracts

Demand an Abstract
Insist Upon Protection
Reduce Your Theft
Insurance

Automobile Abstract and Title Co.

Detroit   -   Chicago

Automobile Abstracts

Contained within the pamphlet, "Automobile Abstracts," it reads, word for word, the following topics and quotes:

Purposes of Organization
1. To issue abstracts of title for automobiles as abstracts of title are now issued for real estate.
2. To eliminate thereby, completely and for all time, the ever increasing traffic in stolen cars.
3. To reduce theft insurance rates by the simple process of destroying the thief's market.
4. To provide all times, upon demand, a guarantee and proof of ownership for the 6,000 automobiles, now in use, throughout America.

Why An Abstract Of Title For An Automobile?
A question most easily answered by another question-why an abstract of title for your real estate? You would never purchase real estate without insisting upon an abstract. Why then an automobile, which frequently represents an even greater sum. A real estate abstract tells you all about a given piece of property, what liens, mortgages, encumbrances of any kind there are against it. It is a complete history of ownership. An automobile abstract does just exactly that for motorcars. Our abstract is a complete and absolute record from distributor to junk pile. Every lien, mortgage, every replaced numbered part is faithfully recorded. A car cannot be stolen and resold when it is covered by an abstract any more than one could steal and sell a house and lot. Imagine what a service we shall perform for manufacturing, distributor, and most of all for motorist.

What Does It Mean To The Man Who Buys?

Just this: it protects and guards his purchase. It gives him a clear and lawful title to his car. A bill of sale doesn't always constitute a clear title. Suppose you purchased a motorcar from a friend whom you knew absolutely to be honest and upright. Suppose the friend himself bought the car from a crooked dealer. Or, to go still further, presume that the dealer himself was victimized when he purchased the car. The dealer would then be in a position of receiving stolen goods and would pass on to your friends and finally to you, a title that had no legal value whatsoever. Very shortly, it would be impossible through the use of abstracts for such a condition to arise. If you wanted a diamond, you would hesitate to enter the average pawn shop to purchase unless you were willing to take a chance and did so knowingly. Yet, hundreds of automobiles are purchased just that way every day.

What Does It Mean To The Buyer Of A New Car?

It means protection for him when he is ready to sell. All new cars become secondhand cars in time and are offered for sale. It means reduction in his theft rates. The distributor will be compelled to insist that every purchase carry an abstract of title with it. That's the only way in which the dealer can protect himself and his good name. Otherwise, he lays himself open to suspicion that he is unwilling to provide his customer with something that customer is going to need and need badly when he sells.

What It Means To Insurance Companies

The practical elimination of the theft problem. At present only 40% of all cars carry any insurance whatsoever, owing to excessive rates made necessary by present conditions. That means six out of every ten car owners who cannot afford insurance will receive the benefits of greatly reduced rates.

Losses In Stolen Cars $75,000 A Day!

A startling condition, truly. Imagine the banks of this country being daily robbed of such a sum! How long would outraged public opinion stand for a condition so deplorable? How long can insurance companies stand the strain?

Listen to Chas B. Disbro of The American Automobile, writing in the National Underwriter of April 24:

"If present conditions continue to grow worse, theft insurance will have to be discontinued altogether." And The Insurance Field, "From official returns made by the various companies coupled with private records submitted... to give a reasonable fair view of the results in 1918, the following deductions have been made:
Liability—Profitable
Property Damage—Profitable
Collision—Fair
Fire—Profitable
Transportation—Profitable
Lightning—Profitable
Tornado—Profitable
Theft—Unprofitable

Of eight classifications only one unprofitable. If there were no other vital all-important reason for an abstract, this fact alone would justify its existence."

Other Far-Reaching Benefits

The actual benefits resulting from the widespread use of automobile abstracts, are so many, so varied, and so altogether novel, that some understanding of them is necessary to acknowledge the company's money making possibilities.

Secretaries of state throughout the nation will find it is a great boon in simplifying clerical work and providing necessary information which they are not now in a position to obtain. Manufacturers will find, in the abstract, the first and only method devised to give them quick and accurate history of their cars once they have passed from the distributor. In the loaning and borrowing of money, the abstract also performs a marked service. Many cars are sold every day with the unsatisfied mortgages and liens against them. This will be no more possible with a car under abstract than it would with real estate. Police departments will also find the abstract of vast service in locating thieves who attempt to sell cars in other states.

Our Nation-Wide Advertising Campaign will soon be launched in page advertisements in every metropolitan newspaper in America. This will be supplemented by an elaborate publicity propaganda which will speedily hammer home to every motorist the necessity and importance of our abstract. An active working force of 50,000 insurance agents, garage owners and distributors will handle our abstracts in every town and hamlet in the nation.

Endorsed By Everyone
No other concern, to our knowledge, enjoys such complete and widespread endorsement of its plans. The Abstract & Title Co. has the hearty support of leading insurance executives, automobile manufacturers, dealers, governors, statesmen, police chiefs, sheriffs, welfare workers and automobile clubs all over the country.

Here are a few, culled from the many:

"I have referred your enclosures to the Hoosier Motor Club with my endorsement."
—George B. Coffin, Chief of Police, Indianapolis, Indiana

"[The Abstract & Title Company]... has my unqualified endorsement."
—J. T. Janssen, Chief of Police Milwaukee, Wisconsin

"I approve of this...and feel that it will practically eliminate automobile thieving..."
—Robert J. Alderice, Chief of Police, Pittsburgh, Pennsylvania

"I have perused contents of your letter...and in that connection wish to state that I am heartily in favor of same."
—Robert D. Carter, Marshall, Baltimore, Maryland

"I think your proposed automobile abstract of title for automobiles is a splendid thing."
—N. F. Johnson, Chief of Police, Portland, Oregon

"After reading over your automobile abstract of title, ... you cannot quote me too strongly as being in favor of same."
—J. Parley White, Chief of Police, Salt Lake City, Utah

"Concerning the stealing of automobiles... I believe it will have a marked tendency to prevent the disposing of stolen automobiles..."
—John J. Garrity, Chief of Police, Chicago, Illinois

"Has my full endorsement..."
—James L. Beaver, Chief of Police, Atlanta, Georgia

"It will put the crooked automobile handler to an awful disadvantage and eventually put an effective stop to the traffic."
—W.W. Rhodes, Chief of Police, Peoria, Illinois

"I beg to inform you that I have taken this matter up with the different garage men and dealers in the city, and they all feel...it would be a mighty fine thing and would be in favor of it. It would certainly be a great help to the department, and save the department much time and annoyance."
—Peter Kline, Chief of Police, South Bend, Indiana

The Prospectus stated:

All The World Prospers.
"Without inconvenience or delay, with an outlay of five minutes in time, and a trivial of two dollars and fifty cents in cost, the American motorist will receive the greatest single benefit he has ever enjoyed for such a minimum of time and money. The cost to the public for the Automobile Abstract of Title and services in connection has been fixed at a fee of two dollars and fifty cents, which are the gross earnings of this company. In connection with the Automobile Abstract of Title this Company will receive a fee of two dollars and fifty cents for each and every time the automobile, so covered with abstract of title, is sold or transferred. The fee includes a Guarantee of Title covering every transaction in the Abstract Document. Our earnings should be twenty million to fifty million or more annually, after deducting the total cost of operation. Think what this will mean to the shareholders of this company. 'Everyone is welcome to become a shareholder,' he stated."

Now in all fairness, can you honestly say this was nothing for nothing at all and by nobody? In reality, does this sound like a harsh and unconscionable deal? Does this sound by any means false, misleading, deceptive or dishonest? If so, why would constituents endorse him with their confidence?

Society at large was behind his business which was thoroughly tested with time and money invested. An official salute was given.

> *"Find something the whole world needs and invest in it."*
> — Hetty Green.

And that my friends, is exactly what Cecil L. Snyder provided.

Cecil wanted the legislature to pursue a standard practice requiring registration of automobiles. His General Counsel for Automobile Abstract & Title Company, Chas E. George, initiated writings called *Desired Legislation*, a purposed law, "a bill to suppress crime and preserve the public peace and safety."

Desired Legislation requested legislation be passed and enforced by state legislatures and stated the reason for this necessity, "to stop the automobile thief." The Automobile Abstract & Title Company was seeking cooperation from the legislature, but instead, became victims of state legislature infringements and finally government usurping.

As a faithful patent holder, Cecil was a trusting soul in his marriage vows with the government. Then a sophisticated session of sensationalism began to take form and shape. The legislature started calling the shots and they yelled, "Hands up Cecil L. Snyder," as his business fell under scrutiny for violating the Antitrust Law, a law designed to regulate the conduct of businesses and corporations, to promote fair competition for the benefit of consumers.

Cecil was not a selfish man. His intentions were pure. He designed this system as a protective service to stop crime, as well as supplying jobs for thousands.

The Automobile Abstract & Title Company had clerical positions starting at fifty dollars per week, which was good money back then. His only raw material was paper, brainpower, pencils, ledgers and typewriters. Cecil had cornered the market on a real service, a necessity of good protection. The Abstract was a *monopoly* of which this government did not want one man to have. But please understand, this classified monopoly had no real tangible product, it only required transactions of paperwork.

So, when the government came along with their jealous eyes, they sized up the fruits of his labor and they realized the enormous revenue potential. It's apparent the government does not wish to take over anything which requires real manual labor because that would probably kill the politicians who seek out these government jobs. It was only after the government realized that any darn fool could push a pencil, that they swooped in, as in *infringement*, usurping his patent rights. They took all that Cecil had worked so hard for away from him, because they could. Being a Sovereign Entity, they could not be held accountable for their infringement.

Cecil stood tall like the mighty oak tree stretching out his branches and welcoming all to his fortress. But, the legislature saw this mighty oak minding its own business and thought, "We should hack that tree down." So, they began to do a real chop job on him, hacking and hacking away at him with their allegations, jail sentences and fines, as well as several crushing legal blows from the grumpy-faced judges in the hallowed halls of our legal system.

It is true, all big discoveries and inventions come from thinkers, someone who has taken the time to follow through investigating the possibilities, someone who has taken the time to do the research. Truly government should play fair, but do they?

Yes, Cecil L. Snyder shocked the world with his great promise and generous salaries and a fair deal. But the stage was set for a systematic take-over. The legislative bodies snatched the whole operation right out from under all involved. Their ugly heads reared up against the Automobile Abstract & Title Company as they began to grind litigations or "The Paper

Caper Plague," as I refer to it. The invasion was set in motion as Cecil's plight began, all because he was instantaneously catapulted into fame and fortune.

CHAPTER 6

The Story Unfolds

Cecil's struggles with the government were in full force when he met Minnie. Cecil was attracted to Minnie because of her fondness for the simple things in life, all due to her rural upbringing. Cecil, with his city slicker accomplishments, concealed his conservative side under his Detroit businessman appearance. He was silent about his business situations with the legislature, for he was already on shaky ground, but that did not stop Cupid's arrows, as the couple stood on the threshold of romance. Together they gave an impressionable appearance of a typical lady and gentleman of the early 1900s.

Cecil, being the proper gentleman in every sense of the word with his gold signature engraved cane, was handsomely attired. He was exceedingly lanky and lean; he reminded one of a grasshopper. With his long arms and legs gracefully dangling from his white cuffed business suits, he would gracefully stride along in the street.

Minnie Graham was shy, sweet and innocent as the new fallen snow. Her natural beauty required no special attention other than soap and water. She was careful to always have her hair neatly pinned, and she applied perfumes with modesty. She would never think of flirting.

Minnie Graham Snyder
1898-1980

Cecil L. Snyder
March 24, 1892 - February 13, 1963

It was the beautiful Belle Isle Park in Detroit, with its water basins full of yachts and the band echoing musical concerts on a starlit night that produced love intentions. Theaters and the symphony with its laughter, brightly colored gowns and the lovely zoo where they communed with nature, all contributed heavily to the only real happy memories in their life.

After two years of successfully swirling Minnie around the great metropolis of Detroit, Cecil finally convinced her that his intentions were honorable and sincere. She no longer resisted his adoring manner and lovingly accepted his marriage proposal and his platinum wedding band.

Their marriage was celebrated by joining hands in the presence of witnesses, typical of Pennsylvania Quaker ancestry, which came from his mother's side of the family. Cecil, a man of common sense and "Common Law" theory and beliefs, practiced what he was taught by his father, a minister of the church. However, Minnie and Cecil did not have a civil ceremony. This was probably due to the fact that Minnie was a Native American Indian, Cherokee, and by law was not a citizen. Indians would not be admitted to full citizenship until 1924. But, that did not stop Cecil's mother and his grandmother from giving their blessings. If Minnie felt any guilt regarding not having a civil ceremony, she buried her feelings in her soul forever. Indians advocated self-discipline and peace. She put great emphasis on this during her whole life and in all her endeavors.

Cecil was driven with ambitions for his business. Minnie remained in the background. Cecil did not share his financial troubles with her. However, neither could have possibly foreseen that their engagement and wedding would soon entwine not only their love but many common miseries lurking on the horizon...miseries that would consequently entangle them in a web of problematic mud raking, leading to the crumbling of Cecil's honest forthright business. He would soon find himself caught up in a political elevator of ups and downs lasting a lifetime. This would become the prelude to the ultimate doom regarding his patents and copyrights and the ultimate doom for his corporation and his business frontier— a doom that would also hit the family home front.

This doom compounded by an invisible prognostication lurking on the horizon, forecasting what no one could have predicted. It was the sudden late 1920s "Crash" which prevailed and overwhelmed the spirit of the people. This black cloud silently hovered.

CHAPTER 7

The Acorn Sprouts from the Mighty Oak

With the rising of the moon and the setting of the sun dividing the intervals of time, Cecil and Minnie became established in the confines of the institution of marriage. One by one, children were delivered as the stork arrived just about thirteen months apart, according to the calendar and the birth records.

I was introduced to my parents Minnie and Cecil on August 20, 1924. In the panic and confusion of my birth, fresh from the womb of my mother, I painfully exploded with a cry, as the family doctor initiated an uninvited smack on my butt.

Mother and Father, after much contemplation, gave me the name, Eleanor Cecilia. Being blond and fair, I duly represented my father's family heritage. I had the Pennsylvania Dutch touch. Thirteen months later, I was joined by a similar counterpart, a baby girl born on September 15, 1925. She was called Velma

Joyce. She stole the hearts of the nurses in the maternity ward with her large brown eyes, rich coloring of skin tones and black hair resembling Mother's Indian heritage. Mother certainly had her hands full, for I was only 13 months old when my infant sister came along.

Following the birth of Velma, a little over 13 months later, Mother once again packed a suitcase to make way to the hospital. She was expecting the birth of a third child. On November 16, 1926, a small sweet fair-haired lad with light skin tones of Father's heritage, plus a likeness to Mother's side, was born and produced happiness, an heir to the family name. He was given the official name Vern Graham Snyder. Father called him Sonny Boy.

Father's timing was not to be reckoned with, for in the following year of 1927, thirteen months to the day, the stork passed over the rooftop again. Grandmother's house was full of infants, and yet here comes another joyful bundle of dependency in the form of a tiny baby girl. She was properly named June Delores.

June was a pleasant combination of both sides of the family and balanced the scale. Our family was now complete. Nevertheless, living with Great-grandmother in her small brick bungalow was uncomfortable, for it was bursting at the seams. There was Great-grandmother who was eighty, Grandmother who was sixty, Father and Mother, and us four children.

Like mother hens they hovered over us. The order of the day was tedious diaper washing, laundry, bottles, bath time, colic, crying and teething. But Mother didn't have to worry about formulas, for we were nurtured with "Horlick's Malted Milk," popular in those days.

Along with our growing family and cramped living conditions, Father's nightmares of business legalities were raining down upon him. Father was doing the best he could to meet those head on. Rents were soaring, and a decent place to rent with four small babies was few and far between. It was evident that the government pressures and lack of privacy at home were being felt. The burden of responsibility for his entire family was mounting. Mother's simplicity, on the other hand, would not allow her to fully comprehend all that was taking place with Father's business. Instead, she would silently assume the full responsibility of caring for us while the legal pace was bringing down suffering. She was alone in her dilemma, for Father's attention was drawn to the company and keeping the business alive.

With all of Father's legalities mounting, he was consumed with concern for his family. His mother and his grandmother, as well as his brothers and their good wives, all had an interest in the Automobile Abstract & Title Company. His business partners, constituents, the stockholders and the lawyers connected with the business, along with the people employed at the company, were foremost in Father's mind. He struggled with the political bodies that one could never put a finger on. He continuously had to confront the next frontal development being forced upon him while the government played their games of "get the grasshopper."

The political bodies were doing everything they could to close down his business offices in Detroit and also in Chicago. Heavy fines and court procedures were taking a toll on his finances. They were bogging him down in a quicksand of allegations. The government usurped his patent and copyright, making him unable to make a living and earn his daily bread. It was an injustice. They did not want my father to be able to survive the suffocation being placed upon his person. You see, legislative bodies are not personally responsible for anything they set out to do. They can get away with any piracy and do it in the name of justice without cost to them.

However, Father was never one to lose faith in the law of probability, although facts would later reveal he had endured more than one human could handle. With inadequacies of funds and resources causing misfortune due to the government flexing their muscle, it was putting a strain on his wallet. He was overflowing with troubles and few smiles.

Taking care of his business affairs required my father to commute back and forth between Detroit and Chicago making contacts. Father needed to attend to more pressing matters in Illinois, so he decided to move Mother and us tiny tots to the town of Chicago. This decision would relieve Grandmother Snyder of the burden of our little tribe.

Great-grandmother was old and needed rest and quiet. She was usually taken with a sick spell, and Grandmother Snyder's small bungalow could accommodate only so much hustle and bustle from babies. So, we boarded the train for Chicago with a huge steamer trunk full of our personal belongings. Never would we see our beloved grandmothers again, a fact that was mercifully hidden from our sight at the time.

CHAPTER 8

Lakeshore Drive

Arriving in the city of Chicago with our trunks brimming full of belongings, Father checked us into the 1400 Lakeshore Drive apartment building. The family settled down in a rich, warm nest on the 21st floor overlooking the skyline and the lake shore along the outer drive.

Father always felt that the best was none too good for his family. Mother, on the other hand, was much more rigidly frugal. She felt the high-rent district was way too rich for our blood. However, Father needed to be near the business. Father's offices in the Palmolive Building were within walking distance.

With the business slump of 1929 being felt everywhere, Mother knew little about finances but secretly felt Father was much too extravagant. It seemed that Father had impulses. When he had a few bucks in his pocket, he would insist on having dinner in the best place in town, Henrici's. This lavish living on expensive restaurant meals rubbed Mother's frugality the wrong way. Mother could not get accustomed to this stylish stress while her peace of mind was being threatened. Instead, she concentrated her attentions on taking care of three little ones and one small infant.

I was the oldest, just five in the year 1929, and weaned from the bottle much too early. I graduated to my thumb. Thumb-sucking was a disgusting habit for a five-year-old, but my parents, who were preoccupied with caring for the smaller babies, and Father, who was gone most of the time campaigning for funds to keep the business functioning, did not provide me with much solace. So, in order to obtain the security I needed, I sucked and sucked my thumb until my flesh was numb. With much concern, Mother admitted that I had habits that were unbecoming a soon-to-be kindergartner.

Living on the 21st floor, the cool winds off of Lake Michigan waters made the window curtains flutter day and night. The cool night breezes captured a chill and initiated a slight cold for all concerned. Baby June was not conditioned to change and an ordinary cold settled in her chest. Mother tried different medications to help my baby sister's condition, but her chest was so full of congestion it was making it difficult for her to breathe. Her tiny nose, full of mucus, oozed periodically. Mother did everything she knew to break up the phlegm in her chest, but the baby did not respond and now she was choking badly.

"ELEANOR! ELEANOR! Where are you? Come quickly. We must hurry!" My beautiful Indian mother was calling me from my make-believe world, the place where my subconscious dwelled daily. My long cumbersome name, "Eleanor" could not be shortened to my liking, not in the realm of possibilities, and wishing would not make it so. I lacked appreciation for this gracious grant given to me by my two forbearers when picking a sensible name. "ELEANOR" summoned up not only a call to attention, but it was a call to arms.

Mother was calling me, as she spoke rapidly to alert me to the urgency of the situation at hand. She told me to get my sister Velma and Sonny Boy, for baby sister was very sick and Mother wanted to go to the hospital quickly. Father was seemingly alerted to the fact that any delays might mean the difference between life and death.

As a young child of five, I was blissfully unaware of the serious nature regarding my baby sister's illness. Her beautifully shaped head, covered with wisps of scattered light blonde fuzz, was burning with fever. Her dear little crooked smile was slippery and full of slobbers, as she lay sweet on her bed of misery. Laying in a semiconscious state, baby June's tiny hands and baby fingers reached out for help, in a fitful attempt to sleep.

Throughout the night, Mother had walked the floor exerting efforts of trial and error to accomplish and encourage some relief for the baby using her knowledge of holistic measures, but to no avail. Her skillful applications of these old-fashioned formulas were limited and produced unsatisfactory results. Mother's Indian herbs were at a disadvantage, and Father's beliefs trusted little to professional doctoring. However, it was becoming more and more apparent that their insufficient efforts would now require pursuing other safeguards.

Father rounded us up from the confusion of romping playfulness. With questioning eyes and wonderment of the situation, I noticed Mother seemed more than commonly worried, she appeared deeply distressed. I grabbed my doll which was my constant companion and confidante. I never strayed too far from her in my life. She was the constant link between my realities and fantasies. I loved my doll very much. She would enhance my daydreaming beyond all imagination and would provide the personification of the real and the unreal in my life. I was keenly aware of all imaginary daydreams, and most of all, what my doll meant to me. I would imagine myself as a grand dame carrying a lavish mink. I would drape her majestically and lovingly across my empty arms and clutch her as a treasure to my bosom. She was my first and foremost consideration. I would turn to her in times of trouble.

"Mother may I take my doll to the hospital, may I, may I?" I implored in a pleading manner, asking my mother for an answer to my trivial request during this urgent and pressing situation. "I suppose," she replied. She seemed to be preoccupied with the necessities of the moment. I could not expect too much concern for my own urgency from Mother without provoking her and was satisfied with Mother's simple, "I suppose."

As the preparations for our departure were being completed, three fidgety little ones occupied themselves at the window overlooking Lake Shore Drive, where the waterfront from the white-capped waves on the shoreline mounted the sides of the cement abutments, slapping the face of the concrete. Everything far below seemed so tiny. I set my imagination in motion and became a pebble lying on the broad sidewalk below, hidden under God's toe. Viewing a pebble at such great distance would be totally impossible for anyone else, but for me it was easy. Equating my smallness with the size of a pebble, I thought of God in the heavens above viewing me from His greatness. I was small, insecure, insufficient, and I felt utterly unimportant. I was at a loss to rise up or reveal my thoughts to anyone. I was in a daze.

Father's nervous pacing and Mother's hurried reciprocal attendance to the circumstances at hand was most confusing. I would much rather stay and play with my doll. Soon Mother would be ready with the baby, and my dedication to daydreaming would be replaced with the reality and the duties taking precedence.

Father helped us into our coats to protect us from the chill of the noonday, for the sun was hiding behind a huge cloud. As we struggled and toyed with Father's patience, he smoothed my brow and Mother neatly parted my sister's disheveled hair. In a few minutes, we would be departing to the mystery place called the "hospital." Not only was this a new word unknown to me, it was also an unknown place for me. It rang with an air of grave complications which were soon to be discovered.

In the week before June had taken ill, Father placed us on a platform, grouped in front of his black box camera, where a large light bulb then exploded in our faces. Father explained, "This is called studio stories for prosperity." The family album contained many unprofessional group pictures which Father had managed to capture with his friendly box camera. However, little did anyone realize that this picture would be the final family picture which included baby June Delores.

INVENTOR ANONYMOUS

Velma, Eleanor, Cecil Junior, Baby June Delores
1929

Father anxiously awaited Mother swaddling the baby for her brief encounter with the outside elements. Lovingly, Mother placed a clean cloth of flannel soaked with a smelly application of some greasy substance about her throat. Full of congestion, the inflammation in her respiratory track made her condition acute. Disturbed from her crib where her breathing was irregular, she cried out in a soft murmur of resistance.

"Come Eleanor, take your sister's hand and get a hold of your brother. The cab is downstairs waiting," Mother commanded. Quickly my short legs carried me forward to the door. Father proceeded to hustle us down the hall and into the red-carpeted elevator. We descended into the lobby below.

The friendly over-solicitous red-coated doorman, with the shrill whistle, was patiently waiting to assist us into the cab parked along the curb. The meter was fully engaged and ticking ambitiously toward its fare, as the cab driver awaited our departure. As we sped toward Children's Memorial Hospital, a wisp of Mother's beautiful brown hair flopped untidily on her forehead. She brushed her hair aside and noticed the same little breeze which disturbed her tresses seemed to revive the baby for a fleeting moment. Calling this to Father's attention, Mother seemed hopeful. A ray of brightness beamed through the atmosphere, as they both pressed for another good sign from the depths of the dear bundle carefully resting in Mother's arms. The gleam only lasted for a second. Her fear called upon panic as little baby June seemed to gasp her last breath. The battle with this bug which had inflicted this terrible plague on her fragile constitution was a constant fight.

As we sat neatly spaced on the velour upholstered seat, quietly and respectfully still, we stretched our necks to view the buildings and people in our journey toward the hospital.

Tenseness was in the air and was felt by all, including the cab driver. Having no control over the circumstances, I clutched my little painted-faced doll to my body. Her soft pliable form of stuffed cotton cushioned my hurts. Father had given her to me when I was oh so tiny, but I could not quite remember just when I had gotten her as a gift.

Arriving at our destination in front of the hospital, the attentive cab driver safely deposited me and my sister and brother on the sidewalk. Father assisted Mother from the cab to the curb and paid in a hurried manner, rushing us inside. A lady in white secured the three of us in an empty waiting room. "Now you kiddies wait here, and the nurse will take good care of you while your mother and I take sister upstairs to see the doctor," Father instructed.

Our parents disappeared from sight down the gray corridor, and we were left to our own resources. Never having been in a hospital before, I was suspicious, curious and interested. I twitched and swung my legs against the chair and stared at my sister and brother. After what seemed like an eternity, a nurse came for us, and we were quickly bustled into an elevator.

Unlike the one at the apartment building, this one was rather shaky and creaked and groaned laboriously toward the upper floor. Slowly the door opened, and I caught a glimpse of several white-garbed individuals rushing past in the hallway. Everybody seemed to be in such an awful hurry, almost as though they were running from each other. The nurse gathered us at her skirt and leaned down to give us instructions. We remained very quiet and still. I sensed that all was not right on this floor. Then I spotted Father coming toward us from the room down the hall. I could see from the worried expression on his face that indeed something was vitally wrong. Father, who was a replica of a tall

Lombardy tree, swept Sonny Boy up in his arms, and I linked my sister Velma to me as I reached for my Father's hand. Velma struggled and pulled back slightly as Father propelled us at a rather rapid pace along the corridor. I skipped along to keep up with Father's rushed pace and giant strides. I was beginning to worry about Mother and our little sister.

Upon entering the room at the end of the hall, where Father had previously emerged; my curiosity was satisfied. Mother was kneeling close to a bed where baby June's limp form lay beneath a tent of transparent paper. With his index finger poised at his lips, Father cautioned us to be completely silent and still. Approaching the huge grotesque tent covering June, I grew cold, and a chill came over my small frame, as I viewed my baby sister lying in a death-like posture. Fear shook me, as I peered into the shiny window tent over her bed and saw her tiny helpless arms and bluish limp fingers on the covers. Her lips were tightly closed.

I imagined that she was just sleeping, but her faint blue skin color was obviously revealing a sudden turn which erupted into a last gasp of breath. Without spoken words or explanation, I somehow sensed in a childish immature way that something terrible was taking place right before my eyes.

Father reached for my hand and placed it on top of the tiny baby fingers clutched in a fist and, although she was burning with fever, her hand was turning cold and lifeless. Then Father placed Velma's hand on top of mine and then Sonny Boy's, who had toddled up to the bedside and reached for something, as if he knew what for.

I glanced upward toward Father's stalwart figure leaning over our huddled group. Tears were welling in the corner of his eyes as one came to fullness and dropped with salty flavor on my upturned face. As the droplet splashed on my cheek, I could hear the muffled sounds of Mother's soft sniffling as she desperately tried to suppress them into a handkerchief. The room was silent except for the teneness and sobbing surrounding June's bed. I was desperately probing the situation for an answer.

A robust nurse bustled into the room and began to press us from the bedside toward the open door where the empty corridor was beckoning beyond. I heard her whisper to my father, in a sorrowful tone, "Very sorry, Mr. Snyder. We did all we could for your little one. There's absolutely nothing further we can do now." It all seemed so final. I paused for a moment on the threshold of the door to sister's hospital room, and I turned back for one last and final brief glimpse of the baby.

I don't quite remember, but somehow we left the hospital with its funny-smelling rooms, its big, empty elevator, its cold, vacant corridors, and its bustling busybodies dressed in white with their silly-shaped headgear. We left our little sister to the groaning noise of the rickety elevator and the care of those strangers who admitted they could do nothing for her, and we never returned.

Upon our arrival back home, our living quarters summed up the fact that June's crib was pitifully empty, and Mother's arms had nothing to hold. My doll seemed willing enough, so I offered her to Mother's lonesome lap. Mother smiled her best smile through her tear-stained face.

Silent conversations began to take place between my parents. They were guarding the details of Father's new predicament. He was without funds to provide a casket or a burial plot for our sister. The untimely death of sister brought instant hardship on Father.

After spending many hours viewing the white-capped waves floundering around below our apartment window and acknowledging my mother's silent stare, Father gathered us to go to the undertakers.

Lo and behold, there was our little baby sister lying in a simple snow-white casket. She was posed like a sleeping angel. In the mystery and darkness of the big, empty parlor of vacant, hardwood pews, Mother seated herself away from the lighted coffin which held our baby sister. With her head lowered near her lap and her face covered, canopied from view by her crocheted hat, I sensed a certain solemn sorrow.

Each in turn, Father lifted us up to view June's remains, as we clung tightly to the rim of the white coffin box until our knuckles turned purple. Eagerly, we drank from the essence of the spectacle with certainty and bewilderment. I could not take my eyes from the scene. All decked out in one of her neat little white dresses was baby June, her lips tightly pressed together. Her lids were still without a flutter, as they had been at the hospital.

I inhaled a sweet sickening odor about the coffin and asked Father, "What is that funny smell about June?"

"It is embalming fluid, and that is the smell of death," he answered.

"What is it for?" I asked.

"It's not something you would understand," he explained.

In brief, fleeting procession, the realities of the moment were being absorbed as we were allowed to touch June's cold person for an instant. I leaned in to whisper a soft and final goodbye to the precious lifeless body, which only a few days before was a flesh and blood live baby girl.

In a typical five-year-old mind, I sincerely believed she would hear my soft farewell. Although I could not fully understand the picture puzzle forming before my eyes, our thoughts were as one.

I knew June was listening to me somewhere in that place called "Heaven" that Mother often spoke to us about.

Then Father turned and approached the undertaker, hoping to explain his predicament. This kindly man listened intently to Father's perfectly legitimate explanation of his financial position and lent a helping hand with credit for the use of the parlor and the small white coffin. Humbly, Father thanked the undertaker for his kindness and assured him that he would do his best to repay him for his service at a later date. After politely shaking hands, the two men parted. The undertaker then arranged for burial in the only plot they could provide and that was in the Potters Field section, in the Rosehill Cemetery. She remains there to this day without a marking or headstone.

June Delores was our sister's name, and she was only with us for a little while. Father thought it most cruel, and Mother felt she was left empty and deprived never to hold her baby in her arms again. It was hardly fair. We had so little time to get to know her.

I tried to relate the actual with the factual, and the picture came pronounced and clear. June slept most of the time, as babies often do, but now she was gone forever in sleep. There was no other baby to fill her place. Her crib lay empty. My doll, with her stuffed painted face, looked quite out of place on baby June's pillow. I could not understand why God had taken baby sister away. Only God is all-knowing and wise, but I'm sure I would not have told you so then.

Overcome with sorrow, time did not permit Father the luxury of mourning or withdrawal from work. Father's forced poverty from the government infringing on his patent created financial problems. And, because there have never been any fundraising associations for the protection of inventors' families who are victims of infringement from governmental bodies, Father had nowhere to turn for assistance. He now would work diligently in the hopes of paying down the hospital bill and funeral expense.

My baby sister's crib would lay empty as monumental reminder during the day. Our peripheral thoughts would carry over into the night. As a family, we had to try to participate in normal functions without pausing to recall too much or reminisce beyond normalcy. We were noticeably empty, but her absence made our thoughts grow fonder. It would be a mighty long time before our sorrows would dissipate.

Minnie Eleanor Graham Snyder,
Velma and Eleanor
Cecil Jr.
Baby June
Lake Shore Drive

CHAPTER 9

A Twinkle-Toed Kindergartner

Still living at Lake Shore Drive, having experienced the death of my baby sister, I conjured up fears which were soon diluted with the onrush of new and interesting things; I was caught up in the wonderful world of other children; kindergarten schooling loomed on my horizon.

As an earnest five-year-old, I became interested in the tipsy teeter-totter, a box filled with what appeared to resemble crushed powdered pebbles, a slippery slide, and chocolate milk with straws inside. I had joined the kindergarten society. Leaving my doll behind was a rather severe and hard decision, but my duties to the outside world were obviously calling. I divested myself of my doll and charged her care to my younger sister, Velma. Developing my skills was more important business. The dividends I received from my brief kindergarten activities began to enrich my life, as well as my father's. He deeply felt that the culture and creativity to which I was exposed were important compensations, for he was always busy in the business world.

Struggling with finances and frustration with his business, Father would never allow his daily endeavors to interfere with my little world or the close relationship we regarded and felt toward each other. His projected inner desires, in future hopes for his oldest daughter, somehow mesmerized him into believing that I could someday become a great toe dancer, possibly in ballet. Whirling and twirling like that capricious twisting top, I was all decked out in full gear trying out with aspiration and a will to achieve. I was undoubtedly the hardest-working, twinkle-toed child in the whole group of toddling tots.

Eagerly, I applied myself to the task of toeing the line. I imagined myself tiptoeing through the toe holds, all for naught. Had my toes been the size of Father's, who knows what I might have attained. Alas, with my Achilles heel, tender toes and weakened arches, I failed miserably to stabilize my equilibrium.

One day, my dear, dedicated teacher informed Father with a staunch, statistical statement about my ill-fated steadfastness and stamina, "Mr. Snyder, I'm afraid your daughter is not particularly cut out for this type of expression of dance." Seems I had failed with family factors that framed my feasibility with flat feet.

The truth was announced, and Father was disappointed of course. "You are probably right. I was mistaken. I honestly felt that it would be a stepping-stone to getting her interested in dancing. There is nothing more desirable for a young lady's training than toe dancing," he explained. The ballet dancer in that day and age was on a pedestal of her very own. Chances for pursuing it further were no guarantee of greatness. I was trying so hard to fulfill desires of wishbone dimension, but

Father would have to settle for fulfillment of his hope in some other endeavor.

I was the oldest, and somehow Father's noticeable lavish attention in my direction caused Mother to think there was favoritism being shown. I was not aware of Mother's biased opinion of unfair competition. Mother seemed to have her opinions, and she would express them freely, using parables and metaphors to get her point across. The resources she provided with her appropriate commands were centered on the things in nature, her repertoire stemming from her Cherokee Indian heritage. "Feathers in the hat, arrows in the heart, pebbles on the beach, stones of gall, faces of sun and moon, green as corn, pipes of peace," were all called upon to relate or correlate her meanings. Her squaw-like tendencies invariably showed at times, in a record breaking manner. The fact that Mother often referred to me as a pebble on the beach allowed me to relate. Seeing how all seek to outshine others from a lonely position, pebbles were sometimes shiny and sometimes isolated.

It was fair to say, I had preoccupations. I enjoyed the land of make-believe. I would lose track of reality again and again. Sometimes, I would withdraw from reality by engaging in habits solely for comfort. I did not have to share my thumb-sucking with anyone. This selfish pleasure launched Mother upon a campaign to destroy my fun. She began dipping and dabbing my whole hand into various vile smelly applications, which were rather distasteful in any combination. This included red pepper, cayenne, Castor oil and even a dip in toilet water; all were futile in discouraging my burning desire to remain faithful and dedicated to my pacifying thumb.

Even the attempts my younger sister and brother made to mimic me, with their mildly, mischievous monkeyshines, failed to shame me. I just plain ignored their attempts to mock me. It was my only defense, for their reproductions were the greatest.

CHAPTER 10

Knock, Knock. Who Might This Be?

As my family continued to struggle along daily with its human problems, we were drawn into Father's business difficulties that he was experiencing but never discussed. Mother, who took care of our daily needs, took us for walks to the park and strolls to the Loop. We would venture over the drawbridge to the Palmolive Building to Father's offices. It was very much a part of our daily doings.

But, as Father's finances were touching bottom, many unhappy days would soon begin to descend upon us. With his resources practically nil, my parents were beginning to ride a living nightmare. Dutiful Mother would keep us busy with activities such as cultural involvements and exposures to simple pleasures. This would allow for us to be involved with the world at large.

Then one day, by surprise, a knock came at the door. It was the hotel management bringing down their wrath. They wanted the rent in cold, hard cash. Father's persistent pleading that he would soon have the rent failed. His promises would no longer unlock the door to our apartment. It was plain and simple; the management would no longer be sympathetic.

Mother was instantly refused permission to remove any personal belongings, not even one single memento from our baby sister, who had recently died. We were leaving with only the clothes on our backs. Without sufficient funds, we soon found ourselves out on the street with nowhere to go.

Busily, Father barked up one tree after another until he found the right one. We ended our frenzied flight in a small hotel room in the Chicago Loop. It was a far cry from the place we called home on Lake Shore Drive. Mother said it was less expensive, two hundred dollars a week, which was a sudden drop.

Being forced from our home, the only home I actually remembered, was a shattering experience for me. I was severed from kindergarten and yanked into another dismal experience that I did not understand.

In prior days, Mother explained how we had lived with Grandmother Snyder in Detroit, but I had no real recollection of those days. Father would attempt to jog our memories by recalling little incidences. But unfortunately, I only had eyes for our apartment overlooking Lake Shore Drive. I had all I could do to remember anything else of the past except June's death.

Detroit, Michigan, where Mother said I was born, where both grandmothers resided, was a faraway place that I did not clearly recall. Before my awakening, at the age of five, there remained four years of dark ages for me. I searched my memory for grandmother, whoever that was, but I could not recall her. A faint essence of an incident, remembering little blurs of people around a table, was somehow there in my past. Mother's comments such as, "That child must have weak kidneys. I don't know what I'm going to do with her," rang clear as a bell in my ears. It was my mother's usual way of excusing my habits and labeling my idiosyncrasies. I sort of remembered my mother making this statement to my grandmother at our last supper we had with her. It was clear that I was shutting out these things deliberately, but I would quickly recall them when my memory was jogged.

I seemed to have a fair share of burdensome worries with having weak kidneys, bowlegs and an intolerable toe for dance. This caused me great distress. I could not find a reasonable explanation for my defects. Being pulled out of the rank and file of school, I chalked it all up to failure on my part, causing me to become self-conscious.

With the outside world sliding into a state of distress, from the onset of the 1929 Crash, I was too young to really understand all that was taking place with the outside world. Mother did her best to provide stability, focusing on our daily care and safety. Many times she left unfinished projects like mending a tear or reattaching a loose button or her own grooming habits until the wee hours of the night. She would wait till we were sound asleep or until our insatiable desires and demands for something new and interesting to hold our interests would keep us quietly occupied. We were constantly in motion, hungry for playing. Mother kept us busy while Father was involved with the world of finance.

Then one day a man in uniform came to the door and took Father away. As sure as the sun rises and sets, faithfully each morning for what seemed like an eternity, we went down to the place called "jail." Father had been arrested.

It was so sad to see my father behind bars. He looked so unhappy. Mother would bring him a clean handkerchief and a pack of cigarettes each visit. This new circumstance only permitted me to cling to the bars and reach for my father's hand. When it was time to go, the policeman separated us until the next visiting day. Mother seemed tired of the routine.

On one particular visiting day, I overheard Mother softly conversing through the bars with Father. She seemed sick. She stated, "I don't see how I can hold out any longer. This has gone on too long." The legislative methods of restricting Father were impacting a perfectly happy family, separating us from our father. Whatever Mother was referring to, or speaking about, was beyond my comprehension. My bombardment of questions only initiated answers like, "You are too young to understand." "No, your father is not coming home soon," and "Nobody knows when this will ever end."

Many weeks passed. Each sunrise brought another day for visiting Father and another day of Mother's worried look of sadness. For a very long time, Father did not come home to us, and I was concerned for Mother who was frantically alone. One morning the sun peeked into our small hotel room. I hopped from my bed to wake Mother. Brother and sister were still asleep. I struggled to climb over to reach Mother's bed next to ours. Mother seemed to be unusually still and quiet. I wondered why she had not stirred when I hit the floor with a thud. As I pulled Mother's hand down alongside of the covers, I sensed something was wrong and unusual. Her hand was limp against the bed and fell onto the floor. "Mother, Mother!" I cried. Hysterically, I ran from the room and down the carpeted halls for help. As I shrieked by, doors flew open and heads popped out.

In a matter of minutes, I had more help than I bargained for. The doctor arrived with his black bag. "Get the stomach pump to that woman quickly," he ordered. "Where's this woman's husband?" he demanded. "Be quick, hurry get those children out of this room," he ordered. I was frantic about Mother's condition. I was not permitted to enter once I had left the room. Some strange older ladies dressed Velma and Sonny Boy and carried them from the room.

There was so much confusion. In the background I faintly heard someone say that Father was badly needed. They did not call upon me for answers. I was silently hoping they would find out that Father was in jail and maybe they would let him go. I could see they were at a loss as to what to do about us children.

After being removed from what some lady softly referred to as "the scene of the accident," we were left with a woman who took charge of our care. It seemed forever and ever and ever waiting for a solution to the current problem. I clung to my sister and my brother and resorted to my thumb-sucking habits. I sucked and sucked my thumb till it was wrinkled and flattened beyond recognition.

If Mother's efforts to eliminate my small habit, that I treasured in troubled times, had been successfully done away with, I would have been a basket case with no source of comfort. Mother had failed miserably with her efforts, including the dark brown socks covering my hands tightly tied around my wrists. I was a regular magician when it came to getting free from any restraints which chained me against my only free form of pleasure. My thumb was a crutch. And with the current things taking place, I surely needed a crutch, as well as security in lavish amounts.

"Where is my mother?" "How is Mother?" "What is Mother doing for so long?" "Where did my mother go?" My questions and curiosities were getting under everyone's skin. I listened at every keyhole and crouched behind the couch, as a cat seeking a mouse, every time the grown-ups engaged in a lively conversation. I hung in the shadows so as to remain anonymous. Would my mother be placed in a box like my baby sister oh so many months ago? Would I ever see my father or my mother again? Everything seemed amiss. I was helpless to solve the mystery.

Then one day I heard a strange lady say, "She sure was lucky that she did not swallow a fatal amount." I thought they must be talking about my mother. *What could my mother have swallowed?* Then I heard the word poison, and I wondered if maybe that was what she had swallowed. *What is "poison"? It must be awful.*

There were no more walks to the park, just waiting and confusion. Endless unanswered questions were the order of the day. Then one day, without notice, this strange lady we were staying with brought us to our father's arms. We raced to meet him, and the tears in his eyes told me that he had missed us terribly. He was so happy to be back once again.

When I asked about Mother, Father replied confidently, "Mother will be fine and up and around in a few days. She had a nervous breakdown." We asked him if he had to go back to that awful jail, and he answered, "No, I am free to stay with you children. Don't worry about that old jail anymore." The matter was hushed from our lips and put to rest.

CHAPTER 11

The Cold Reality Sets In

Father looked for a different place to live, and Mother slowly got better. Father commented many times that the business was very bad and that we owed back rent. The banks had closed their doors because of the "Crash." We owed some back rent, and the rent was due again. The banks closed with the people's money locked inside. People everywhere were up against the same condition or so Father said. Father, who always spoke softly, said, "There is no money, no food and no shelter." One day we would eat from a paper bag, and the next day we had none. We were always hungry. What a strange world this was.

Father explained that he was doing his very best to get on with things, but Mother seemed impatient. We needed shoes and warm coats and Mother said her dress was getting shabby. Death, disappointment and despair failed to deter Father's constant bloodhound-like instincts from being derailed. He had an extraordinary skill when pursuing promise and was determined in his efforts to provide us with these necessities.

However, when fall changed to winter and the virgin snowflakes danced down with their cold, cold hearts, lining the ledge outside our window, we still had no proper winter attire to wear, to play outside.

With the rays of sunlight streaming through our hotel window, another sad day came upon us. There wasn't enough money to buy a bag lunch. Father began to take stock of our small personal semi-valuables in our possession. It had been days since he had carried his own cane engraved with Cecil L. Snyder on the gold band. "Best we cash it in for something to eat," he remarked. He was thinking that he might be able to obtain enough money for one paper bag lunch and maybe a loaf of bread or cheese.

He gathered together his personal articles leading him to dismantle his essentials that completed his ensemble of a proper business gentleman. His rather severe sacrifice did not seem to interfere with his preconceived plan to hock whatever necessary for survival.

Among his gathered items were his cufflinks, tie bar, jeweled stickpin and his faithful pocket watch. He claimed it was originally his father's. In a rather reluctant manner, he approached Mother. She seemed to know what he was about to do. Many times I thought Mother was a mind reader. Humbly, Father reached for her loving hands and without a spoken word, he twisted the steel gray platinum band from her finger. Mother's ring slid slowly into Father's palm, as he reached for it like a drowning man fumbling for a life preserver. When Father made a gesture, it was not unusual for Mother to respond in a soulful manner, rebelling was never on her agenda. She obediently and humbly refrained from making any remarks. I knew Mother loved Father deeply, and their background did not invite any outbursts. Father was gentle in dealing with Mother's concerns, and she accepted his good intentions even though at times she would say, "He's too deep for me."

I was just a little over the age of five, but I knew what the adornment of a ring meant. It was a symbol of deep love that my parents had for each other. I could not understand a world that kept stripping Mother and Father of their belongings; a world that would keep us from having a permanent place to live. I did not know why we had to keep worrying about our clothes or where our next meal was coming from. I just could not get the hang of this outside world.

Glorious promises of what the future would be if only a little more patience would be administered, was Father's avid prescription for a better climate, even when situations were in chaos. Father cast himself as a knight in armor, even if it was only momentary. He would say, "Fear not, tomorrow is another day."

Padding his pockets with the assortment of belongings, he proceeded with his decision. I was the chosen one to accompany him on his treasure hunt. We took a short walk into the bowels of the crowded Loop area, to a little store called the "Pawn Broker." Upon entering the little establishment, I looked around in wonderment. I obediently stood near my father's coattails and glanced up to view my father's tall skyscraper figure, as we stood waiting for the proprietor. My neck ached with sudden kinks, as I peered into my father's soft, gentle, kind eyes. He winked at me in a sly manner. We were in the mutual admiration club.

It was a swell old shop full of surprises incorporated with a mildly musty, downright dusty atmosphere. It was packed to the ceiling with almost any kind of item imaginable. At first there seemed to be no one about the shop, for all that met the eye was the profusion of items which comprised the establishment.

From the rear of the store came an old bent man with thick glasses positioned down near the end of his ski-hooked nose. In a way it was bigger and bolder than Father's nose and much uglier. Father's nose leaned over to one side, possibly from his constant habit of wrinkling it because of his postnasal drip. The old man's pock-marked complexion looked like open bubbles in pudding. He had a giant wart hanging under the edge of his nostrils, and it was huge.

I was taught never to point or be critical of others' defects. Father and Mother advocated good manners. However, I had all I could do to resist the temptation of turning these thoughts over a time or two in the private chambers of my mind.

The old man cleared his throat for attention and began to speak rather rapidly in a dialect I had never heard before. His twisted, broken English was very bad, and I could not understand what he was saying. Father approached the man and spoke to the old fellow in a respectable, engaging voice. "Sir, would you be so kind as to make a decent wager for my securities I have placed before you." Father had positioned his collection carefully on the old man's counter. In a slow, indecisive way the man reached for the articles and examined a couple of them under his long protruding eyeglass. Father leaned closer to the counter. His attention was intense as he waited hopefully for a reply. Father injected another pointed statement, "I would be most grateful to you, sir, if you could see your way clear to place a couple of dollars in my hands, for I will redeem my valuables as soon as I get back on my feet. That may take only a week or so from now, if all goes well." Father always believed in the promise of tomorrow, and he lived by it.

THE COLD REALITY SETS IN

The bent man began to speak, "Vell, I'em twying to figger vat I cud giff dat voud make a great differrunce eder vay," he said. "I kenn not giff zoo much, but it ezz da mater ov da golt. Dat izz zoo little golt dat it izz not wort a dang ting."

Father began to reason and dicker with the old man, while I satisfied my curiosity by peering around the darkened shop. It was a glorified junk store, for in a way it held the contents of the poor. I would have loved to explore and rummage to my heart's content, but I realized this would be out of the question. From where I was standing, I could see a glass counter displaying clusters of precious stones, odd jewelry, brooches, medals and rings. There were guns, suitcases with worn labels of foreign cities, fancy hats with large, feathered plumes, clothing hanging from hooks, as well as swords of battle long since passed, all scattered about in his messy-looking store.

As I stood there, I contemplated with much concern what the old man had said in his broken tongue. *What did he mean by that remark, "Dat it izz not wort a dang ting"? Did everything that was worth anything have to be made of "golt"? What was golt, anyway?*

While Father was still trying to bargain for a fair amount, I was busy looking around and pondering. The two of them were trying to come to terms. I could not for the life of me figure out why anyone would not want those lovely, precious things which belonged to my parents.

A few decisive moments later, Father thanked the old gentleman and turned to locate my whereabouts. The old gentleman started talking to the ceiling and waving his hands in a kind of protest. Evidently, he did not like whatever it was he had decided upon and was in a great hurry for Father and me to make a hasty departure before he changed his mind.

Whatever it was that my father received, he was grateful and politely thanked the old man before exiting the door. I skipped along beside Father, as we headed in the direction of our rented hotel room. This was the start of the lean years, and it was going to take more than brain surgery to cheer Mother up, for her mind was loaded with worry.

"For goodness sakes, what detained you for so long?" Mother cried. She was anxiously waiting. Cheerfully, Father patted her on the shoulder and made an offering to her. "Come now Mother, let's get these children fed, and then we'll all feel better." Father was inviting us to eat. "How about a nice roast beef dinner complete with shoestring potatoes and a nice dish of ice cream?"

We all screamed, "Ice cream, ice cream!"

Momentarily, Mother smiled sweetly, and then suddenly she frowned at Father's decision to go to "Henrici's." "You know, Cecil, we just can't afford that kind of place. We don't have the means to pay the rent. How can we afford a meal in a place like that?" Father turned and responded, "Forget the means. Money doesn't last forever. Besides, I have enough for a good hot meal, which will do us all good, and enough left over for a rent payment."

"After that, then what?" Mother questioned.

"Let me worry about finances," Father assured her.

Father was adamant and weakened Mother's common sense. Father made his decision most desirable with his delusions of grandeur. Eagerly he rushed all around to get ready for the proverbial feedbag in the fancy domain of Henrici's. It was Father's favorite dining place.

Father was no doubt exercising a judicial prerogative, and away we went to the castle of uncommon cuisine with our rag bag clothes clinging to our backs. It was just no use having stalled

THE COLD REALITY SETS IN

talks with the man of the house. When one is extremely hungry, the meal plan is a joy to receive, and eating from an old brown lunch bag in a hotel room for too long was getting old really fast. It was plain that many would accuse Father of having no respect for money, but nothing could be further from the truth. He highly respected money, but he had more respect for hunger.

Eating in a terrible restaurant where food was impossible to digest was not the order for that day. Father liked to pamper his extremely weak stomach once in a while. So, we enjoyed the supreme delights of uncommon cuisine under the mammoth famous painting hanging serenely on the back wall of this famous restaurant. The whole matter faded into a memory, and we returned to the realities of the wretched world with all its money problems. We were a family together clinging to happiness which was not abundant during these terrible times. Our lack of funds echoed un-splendid things without an ounce of promise.

Now I suppose Mother, with her Cherokee Indian temperament, toyed with how successful she would have been at trying to change Father's decision-making choices. However, she would hold him accountable for our uncommon situation regarding decisions he made concerning the government. These particulars were not at her disposal. Being Indian and deprived of rights was a way of life for her, but for Father it was a new frontier that he was facing.

Father's stick-to-it determination spoke of the good days to come and how we must look ahead and anticipate. He would indulge out loud, telling us children about the many plans he drew on paper, of the office building he would someday build, "all made out of colored glass." His many drawings led me down the corridors of his dreams.

In the evenings, he stirred our imaginations by saying, "Someday we will go down to Marshall Field and buy you each a doll of much better quality." He spoke of how remarkable the new dolls were, and of course he had no trouble finding an audience for this type of speech. We were there to hop on his lap at a moment's notice.

Father believed sincerely in these truths with all his heart, otherwise he could not have been so convincing. It wasn't a mere act. I sensed Father could almost taste, reach and smell his dream. He thought the possibilities were on the horizon. From his standpoint, standing in the middle of his mirage, it was just around the next corner. Looking back through the telescope of time under a high-powered magnifying lens, one can now see just how remote his hope was. Hard work and optimism was not the answer. It was his blinding faith and philosophy that drove his supernatural desire. He was merely human with his heroic thoughts and dreams. His never-ending strength overshadowed his human performance. He had a pocket full of dreams and promises, but in reality it was a future full of manholes manifesting.

CHAPTER 12

The World Keeps Turning

Father's predictions were wrong and prosperity was not around the next corner. Instead, the black clouds of tragedy were hovering and gathering overhead. Great-grandmother had passed away in Detroit. At the age of 82, she was called home to God. Grandmother Snyder was now alone and ill.

Immediately, Father left for Detroit to make the funeral arrangements. Utilizing what funds were left from the sacrifices from our pilgrimage to the shrine of the pawn broker, Father placed a small, pitiful amount in Mother's frugal hands.

Great-grandmother was very old, and Father loved her dearly. She had been a second mother to him. He spent the greater part of his early manhood basking in her loving care. The death angel had once more passed over Father's haunted existence, like a dreadful spirit, never allowing him to be free from its cold reality. Father had faced death when June died. Her sweet pure soul had been snatched from the very beginnings of life itself. She was not quite two years old. Great-grandmother was quite the opposite. She had lived a long, morally good existence dictated by her puritanical background. In Father's eyes, she had an ample share of the good life. Yet, Father's reflections of prior happy reunions were shrouded in misery. He would now need to call on his inner strength. No one would deny Great-grandmother was a gallant lady, least of all Father.

In my mind, this funeral was the same dismal, silent, tearful happening that had entered into our lives when baby June died. I felt sorry for Father. He seemed to always be in a hurry as he raced from one disaster to another. First it was his daughter, then he almost lost my mother while he was in jail, and now Great-grandmother was gone, truly a stinging slap in the face.

The world seemed to always be snatching at people's lives and taking a chunk here and a chunk there. Mother always said we must be thankful for what we have. To me, things and people were disappearing fast, and we really had little to be thankful for, but Mother would say that responding with bitterness was not the way to act.

Soon after Father's departure, I entered first grade. I liked school, but I did not have stable circumstances to have any confidence. Our way of life was filled with uncertainties. I never knew if my home would be there when I returned from school.

While attending school, I discovered my love for reading and penmanship. I became an avid practitioner of my father's methods of writing. His handwriting was the most bold and beautiful that I had ever seen, as well as unusual. Father had purchased a slender pamphlet on the correct designs of the art of writing calligraphically. Skillfully, I copied the swirls of oval successive movements with wrist windups. Funny blobs of ink would splatter and speckle my nice, neat paper. Father always applauded my efforts and would remark, "Someday you can be my secretary and work in my office. You show much promise, but you will need lots of practice." While Father was gone, I applied myself diligently, hour upon hour, copying Father's handwriting style, so that when he returned I would have good results to display.

In order to practice my penmanship skills, I would go to the lobby desk and collect the hotel envelopes, which I found interesting. I would address them to some faraway place. Father's business mail came from all over the United States, so I had a wide selection to choose from. I practiced addressing envelopes and proceeded to mail them out with pretend postage. Somehow, they got to their destination in spite of obvious handicaps, for when Father returned he had the same familiar envelopes in his vest pocket, the ones that I endeavored to mail without assistance. Father found this highly commendable, and it made his day.

There was no doubt, my Father was proud of my resourcefulness. I had an insatiable desire to learn, and I was a voracious reader. I learned quickly; things came easily for me with very little effort on my part. Father would select books for me, but I memorized the words so fast that Father felt that it was of little challenge for my inquisitive mind.

Mother never understood my never-ending thirst for knowledge. All she seemed to see were my faults that not even Indian prayer beads could change.

Yes, my mother's background was lacking in formal education, but whatever she lacked in education she made up for in beauty. She never resorted to artificial paint on her face; Mother was crowned with natural beauty, saucer brown eyes, bushy brows and alluring lashes. Her hair always smelled clean and was neatly pinned behind her head with hairpins, in a biscuit-like shape at the back of her head. I was in awe of her great beauty. I worshiped her quiet majesty from across the room.

I dreamed of someday having tresses like Mother, for my hair was curly. Combing sessions were not rewarding. These trial-and-error sessions ended in frustration for everyone concerned. When tangled snarls met with Mother's comb, it became too tiring for her. One afternoon, while Father was at work, Mother sponsored a scalping session, and we were the scapegoats. When Father came home and saw that our hair was cut beyond repair, he could not conceal his displeasure. He just shook his head and commented, "This is regrettable," and that was as far as it went. Father adored long hair, but Mother could not stand the struggling sessions anymore.

Despite Mother's barbering skills, Father would insist on all of us being impeccably groomed no matter how financially depleted we were. It was a tedious task to keep us clean and neat, especially when we had so few changes of clothes. Father had only two shirts, and these needed to be laundered. This laundry service was penny reasonable. Father also needed to have his patent leather shoes shined, but he could not afford a nickel to have them done on a regular basis. So, he cleaned them with Vaseline and wore his spats to cover up the need to have a shoeshine.

Before money got tight, I would many times accompany my father when he went for his customary and regular shoe grooming ceremony. I would climb up on the high seats which were used for this purpose and sit down beside my father. He would then place his long legs against the iron props. The shoeshine man would snap and crack at Father's shiny black toes, sometimes missing them altogether. Shining shoes properly was an art, and the shoeshine man incorporated much skill in his effort, along with his friendly whistle and polite "Thank you sir."

It was a pleasure for me as a child to accompany my father, whether it was for a shoeshine or a trip to his office building, prior to the business slump. There I discovered the shiny spittoons positioned along the side of the desks in the offices. These shiny brass receptacles were a necessity for men who chewed tobacco. They also made a swell place for finding one's reflection and a good source of entertainment.

While sitting at a desk with my legs dangling down, I would try to locate myself in the slanted inverted rims of the spittoon. These hallucinatory reflections would produce themselves in an upside-down position. There I viewed my distorted mirror image, which loomed with a grotesque face toward me. If I leaned away and then back toward this metal pot, my image would lose its expression completely.

This was fascinating for me and provided amusement, occupying my time while I waited for Father to complete his business session. These terrestrial trips into my subconscious were sometimes referred to by my mother as "going into a fog," another famous saying of hers. She could produce them at will. Her actions might lead one to suspect she was dull and spiritless, but her lack of animation was only because she was suffering from worries directly connected with Father's business affairs. She tried to remain focused on the needs of family, using whatever survival skills she could muster up, to keep her from suffering from crisis, on any given day.

Most of the time, Mother displayed a melancholy demeanor. Seldom did she raise her voice, but she was firm in her decisions. We knew just how far we could push before blast-off occurred. Extreme silence meant she was deeply concerned. A happy hum meant she was in a good mood. If our play got too rough, it would result in Father warning us to, "Watch out, you know who is in a bad mood today."

Our parents were extremely different in their mannerisms toward us, both in discipline and rewards. Mother would rock the youngest child if a rocker was available, but we were never permitted to crawl into her lap. The other side of the coin was Father who never rocked us ever, but would allow us the freedom of crawling all over him during play. We used it lavishly whenever the occasion presented itself.

The following days were quite lean. With our world in such a disastrous state, the people were running in circles just trying to survive the state of the economy due to the onset of the Depression. We were no different.

Soon, a chain of events began to evolve which seemingly predicted a gloomy future. With the memory of the recent funeral still clinging in the air, it seemed like the wolf was constantly at our door. The landlord would come pound on our door demanding the rent with repeated warnings. Our lack of ability to pay was calling for wizardry on Father's part.

As a child of six, I knew very little of how "rent" was obtained. Mother would comment, "Your Father is a bullhead," an interjected statement of wisdom that I could not relate to. It was puzzling. One day we had food and a place to live, and the next day no food and the rent was always due. Father was flanked with worry, but he never allowed this to get under his skin. He had a marvelous way of retrieving us from the brink of disaster. His cliffhangers were timely. Confrontations with landlords would either place us in a negative position, with a few more things going to the landlord as collateral, or we would be in a positive position and obtain some small thing from the hock shop. We were down to Mother's gold in her teeth. Father was reluctant to stoop to this, but Mother willingly offered. It seemed gold was the only thing available to attract the commodity of money from thin air.

Father never discussed or explained his financial situations, but with a snap of his fingers he conveyed messages of hope to Mother when she became distressed. His promises would predict a hope of a rosy future. Even I would develop dreams of my own with Father's contagious sprinkles of dreams and moonbeam ideas.

However, Mother expressed doubt and showed her dissatisfaction with her silence. Her wise philosophy would be howling clear regarding the family situation. She felt that Father's promises were only producing holes in his pockets and half soles on his shoes. On the other hand, Father took the outlook that anyone could get new shoes and thought that one should remember the man without feet.

This way of life, being snatched from schools, moving numerous times without any in-depth explanations, left me with some confusion. In reality, these things transpired because of Father's resources, or lack thereof.

CHAPTER 13

Moving On

With the crushing weight of poverty pressing down on all of us, it was becoming unbearable for Mother. To her, Father's financial business difficulties would place conditions on us that would impact all our lives. At times, Mother was unyielding and silently touchy. She did not share her thoughts with anyone. Together, my parents were being swept along by gravitational forces beyond their control as the legislature continued to bring financial ruin down upon our family.

When Father was out of town on a business trip, Mother would remain cloistered in our rented hotel room. With the walls closing in on her, day in and day out, she was beginning to feel the pinch in her moccasins, so to speak.

All hotel rooms looked alike in those days. Each room decor, with flavors of the past tenants, left nothing much to amuse or delight anyone, especially small children. We didn't even have a radio. A public place of accommodation for travelers was anything but paradise for a permanent guest, especially one with three small youngsters. The house detectives would roam the halls to furnish protection. It was necessary to keep the doors locked because of strangers. These long hallways became enticing runways for us children. However, our antics were met with much displeasure from some tenants who were trying to get some sleep.

If weather permitted, we would be treated to a long walk in Grant Park, near the Loop. Sometimes, we went to the beach to play in the sand. Upon our return to the hotel room, we would play games at the hotel window. We would count cars and point at people as they trotted back and forth below us on the street.

These days would become trying for Mother, who couldn't keep up with the business situations. We never fully realized what our parents were going through. They wisely shielded us from the harm which could have resulted.

Then one day, not long after my great-grandmother's funeral and one of Father's business trips, the landlord called Father for consultation. It was about being over-extended with his credit. No longer could the management wait. We owed rent and must go. We packed what few belongings we had and quietly left the dingy hotel for a place on Wilson Street.

It wasn't long after we moved that Father was arrested again. This time the story hit the evening paper. His picture appeared on the front page like a common criminal and loomed blatantly big. Father said, "I am a businessman not a criminal. The politicians and the government have for too long been having a war on business. At one time they did all they could to help businesses. But now, they seem to think they should have complete control over businesses. They are strangling the life blood from this country."

Father would serve his sentence. Upon his return from jail, I searched for visible scars, but there were none to be seen. In spite of his bad publicity, Father was able to obtain credit once again and replenish his funds in small denominations. His friends faithfully and frequently came around giving him their support. Day and night he worked very hard, striving to take care of what there was left of the business.

When time permitted, Father's relaxation centered on us children. We thought he was wise and wonderful. In our eyes he was a different kind of great warrior. With his endless imagination of fairytales and nursery rhymes, it delighted us simple children, who desired his attention. It was his favorite armchair sport.

When we climbed upon his lap, he would entice us with bedtime stories. Mother, who had mixed emotions of delight and displeasure, fully appreciated keeping us occupied, but she frowned upon any lengthy nighttime stories that would keep us up past our bedtime.

There was little doubt that Father was anything other than a family man, and he proudly displayed his little tribe on every occasion which presented itself. As I look back now, I vividly remember the many times I went with him when he sought out extensions of credit. I believed he felt my presence was a good endorsement for his sincerity. People gave with their hearts. I know they must have felt sorry for Father. Never once did he fail to convey to them his sincerity, and they seemed confident in his business venture. The credit style of living was basically and probably the only way we were able to survive. I know he was appreciative of their generosity.

With the many attempts the government made to take Father down, causing him financial drain, he never deviated from his steadfast determination to put the business back on track.

It wasn't until after the federal agents had detrimentally raided his offices that total devastation occurred. Many people lost their jobs. From eyewitness reports, complete and utter destruction took place. Typewriters were bounced on the floor, papers and ledgers were scattered and ripped. The place looked like a bomb had been dropped. At that time, Father was completely overwhelmed by the destruction and demanded an explanation. He wanted an accounting from the "silent halls of justice," but none was forthcoming.

Because of this total devastation and glaring bad publicity, many animosities prevailed. Misunderstandings developed and frightened stockholders demanded their money back as they withdrew their support. Several filed suit in court for return of their holdings. On the other hand, there were many, many more faithful friends who understood what was taking place. They knew Father well enough to trust in him. They knew Father's financial jam was directly due to the government's fines and jail sentences levied on him.

There were no more offices. Never again would I go with my father to the Palmolive Building where the shiny spittoons decorated the aisles. Never again would I glide in and out among the swiveling chairs, proudly sporting my mammoth hair bow hidden behind my head.

Father's problems were enormous and soon to be compounded by the need to find shelter once more, for Mother was now big with her fifth child and the rent was overdue. Father was put to the task again. We were transplanted to my aunt's home in Maywood. Our great necessity caused overcrowding in her dwelling, but because we had no money, we needed to call upon her good charity. Mother would now prepare for an at-home birth. I was not fully informed as to what was about to happen.

The excitement of a new baby and the transition to our new home found me totally unprepared.

Meanwhile, Father and his business associates were preparing to go to court with their first patent infringement case. How they mustered the money for this confrontation is beyond comprehension, for we were flat busted with no means for clothes or food.

CHAPTER 14
I Owe I Owe.
It's Off to Court We Go

Below is what is recorded in the court records:

Re: Patent 1,433,975(Infringement)
Copyright No. 491,492
Cecil L. Snyder

Automobile Abstract & Title Company
Vs.
Haggerty [Secretary of State of Michigan]

Secretary of State of Michigan, No. 4485, District Court, Eastern District of Michigan, Southern Division, decided *on January 10, 1931, the written decision of this court is reported in volume 46, of the Federal Reporter 2d on page 86.*

The decision was that there was no provision to sue the state and therefore no state official could be held responsible for any ruling. *The case was dropped.*

Soon after this court case, on February 2, 1931, Mother presented Father with another dependent. Born on Groundhog Day, a tiny little red papoose-type baby girl was delivered in this little three-room-flat where the seams were already bulging from too many youngsters. No name was given to new baby Snyder. Because it was an at-home delivery, there was no need to hurry.

Around this same time, Father made the acquaintance of a new friend, Mr. Honer. He owned a wholesale grocery business in Maywood. Mr. Honer and his wife, being charitable Christians, took an interest in Father's business. They also took an interest in the family and offered an empty house which they owned, to let. They proceeded to help out by supplying food and medical care for Mother, who was still weak from giving birth, and for our new baby sister, who was half starved before she was born. Without the necessary blankets and clothes, the baby was only swaddled until Mrs. Honer managed to supply a few needed essentials.

Mother feared the worst when the baby became violently sick. But proper medication, warm milk and blankets helped to avert another disaster. In Mother's garden of confusion she felt she was a burden but was most grateful for their assistance.

Poor but proud, our new baby sister was the center of our new joy and happiness.

Mother explained that this new little "Miss no name," was sent to replace our other sister, baby June. Unlike June, who had soft, white, fair skin, blue eyes and a crooked smile, this baby had a red, wrinkly face. She was covered with black fuzz and had eyes of coal, with a mouth way too large. I envisioned another hungry mouth to feed. I overheard my mother say, "We certainly don't need another baby at this time, but if the good Lord wills it, so be it."

The following month, Father launched another attack against the government and their infringing.

>Automobile Abstract & Title Company
>Vs.
>Fitzgerald

>Filed March 30, 1931, in the same federal court. No. 4714

>The court's opinion in this case is not reported. This case was then appealed to the Federal Circuit Court of Appeals for the Sixth Circuit, which is located in Cincinnati, Ohio. The appellate court merely issued a brief decision reading "Degree of District Court Affirmed" on April 6, 1933, No. 6204, and reported in 64 Fed (2d) 1008. A petition for a writ of certiorari was then filed in the United States Supreme Court, asking that Court to hear the case. However, it declined to do so in a brief decision stating "Certiorari Denied," No.47, on October 9th 1933, as reported in 54 S. Ct.48, 290 U.S. 628, 78 L. Ed.547. The

result is that the decision of the lower federal court was sustained and the suit was dismissed.

Apparently this second suit against Fitzgerald was on the same basis as the first suit against Haggerty. In the first case, the court's written decision is published so we could determine what the case was about, the legal theory on which it was based, and the reason why the court made its decision to dismiss. It was a suit of equity against the Secretary of State of Michigan for an injunction to prevent further infringement and damages for past infringements. The court held this was, in effect, a suit against the State of Michigan, that a sovereign state cannot be sued without its consent, and that it had not consented to be sued in that case; also, the 11th Amendment of the Constitution would bar such a suit in federal courts.

The lawyer who did the research for these two cases said these decisions were buried in the finest print of some old law books and that he had a very hard time finding them at all. Most of the original lawyers, who handled this case, are now dead. As much as one can figure out from the record, there were many lawyers who worked on this case against the government, but to no avail. Much work, time and badly needed money, which could have been used for food, clothing and shelter, went into getting these cases to court. The government had made its final decision. They saw dollar signs and wanted this for their own revenue treasury box.

Fines and court fees for cases such as this are extremely beyond the ordinary man's resources. Not even great corporations can survive the purge when government presses punitive laws and is ambiguous in its penalties. Its administration does not encourage patience. The torture of the delays and the interpretations of patent laws along with the injustices of courts with the many diversified ideas and rulings of the judges is what it is all about.

The delays and expense of patent infringement challenges have been a big problem for individual inventors, whose rights should take precedence. But do they, when the government infringes? The assurance of a just and fair trial is lacking.

These events and legal expenses were extremely problematic. If it were not for the Honers' kindness, Father would have had no place to conduct business. They financed setting up an office for him in the LaSalle Hotel in the Chicago Loop. Then one day, Mr. Honer called Father for consultation; he was troubled. He told Father his store customers were unable to pay their bills. He said he would be forced to quit loaning further money to safeguard them from threat of foreclosure.

When Father returned home, he found the family quarantined with scarlet fever; the Health Department had tacked a red warning sign on the door, "Keep out." He was forced to find refuge elsewhere for two weeks.

During this time, Father, who had been given a necklace as a donation, thought that maybe Mrs. Honer could give him some money for the necklace. The Honer's financial situation put them in a predicament. Mrs. Honer could only spare a few dollars, even though Father requested more. Father became angered with frustration. He felt the Honers were letting him down and left an angry note for Mr. Honer, who was not there at the time. Father then proceeded to the grocery store across the street.

When Mr. Honer returned, he read the note that Father left. He became very upset and immediately sought out Father for confrontation. When Father emerged from the other store carrying a bag of groceries in his arms, he was confronted by Mr. Honer, who was usually a calm man. He was waiting on the curb with fire in his eyes. He stood up and grabbed Father by the neck and tossed him into the street. His plump slightly five-foot-tall figure displayed the strength of ten men. Father's groceries were spewed along the street sewer, with potatoes and onions flying in the air and down the gutter.

Mr. Honer, kindly Mr. Honer, was furious with Father and deeply hurt, for he cared for our little family. Father humbly picked himself up and proceeded to soothe Mr. Honer's temper. He then realized what his note had wrought. After a simple explanation and a necessary apology, Father assured Mr. Honer that things weren't too bad. They both composed themselves and regained their equilibrium, as Father assured and convinced Mr. Honer, "things will be underway shortly."

This time Father was right, and it wasn't long before people began to get interested again. Campaigns for funds for his new reorganization began to take shape. Money started to come in slowly from friends and from interested backers. Things were starting to look up.

CHAPTER 15

Lightning Can Strike Twice

Timing is everything they say and tragedy is no different, for it was approaching fast on the dark horizon. A telegram announced Grandmother Snyder's death. Father's face showed wrinkles of strain as he held back the impact of this sad news. If this bad news wasn't enough, there was more in the making.

Father, who was preparing to leave Chicago for Detroit to attend his mother's funeral, would be told that contractors who were working on his mother's home caused some severe problems. They were not bonded and could not be held accountable. This bungling from the contractors, as well as the heavy investing she did in Father's business, caused her home to go into foreclosure.

Father's business had mounting legal fees, and the money that could have been used to repay his mother and his brothers for their investing was spent elsewhere. This caused animosity between them. Father did try to straighten things out in Detroit, but it only led to direct confrontations. His explanations never did bandage the wounds. Father was troubled by this, so when he returned he was determined to get the business back on its feet by putting his shoulder to the grindstone.

Around this same time, Mother placed me in school, but I was only there for a very short period of time. While enrolled, my teacher discovered that I had an amazing reading ability. She would use me as a monitor while she left the room to go to the principal's office. I would sit at her desk in front of the room and read from a book to the class. I was not fully aware of my own abilities, and these occasions made me flush with embarrassment.

Then suddenly my schooling was canceled. We were moving from the Honers' rental back to the city and the confines of another hotel room. Mother thought it most unbearable. She did not look forward to another hotel. She knew we were getting bigger and far more active and that our adventurous explorations might lead to complaints with the hotel management. Sure enough, we were forbidden to run through the hallways and ride the elevators alone. The only place we had left was the basement, where most of the hotel workers gathered for coffee. These hard-working people understood our circumstances and allowed us to visit their domain.

In the basement was the furnace room which had waste shoots that belched bundles of wonderful magazines. We would scurry to gather the bundles like playful pack rats and carry them back upstairs to Mother. There I would read to my sister and brother. The wealth of knowledge I obtained was directly due to the junk other people had thrown down the chutes. Mother provided me with scissors so I could make cutouts of characters from the magazines. I animated my own cartoons and shared with my sister and brother the art of imagination. This talent was imparted to me early on from Father's storytelling. I knew how to dramatize and entertain myself. I could turn a dull hotel room into a land of make-believe in order to relieve myself of the stress and strain of daily pressures.

Mother would attend to our new baby sister who was presenting some problems. Many times at night, there would be a gentle rap at the door from someone inquiring about the noise. Mother tried to impress on Father's mind that a hotel room was not the ideal place to raise babies. It was impracticable and most uncomfortable.

Kids can be demanding, and Father tried to relieve the pressure when he was around. He would choose ideal times to take us for a walk to the Loop to view the skyscrapers and point out the Lindbergh Beacon on the Palmolive Building, where his offices were once spread out on the upper floors. Father loved the outdoors and the strolls we took together around Buckingham Fountain and along the lakefront. This time brought us closer together. The bridges, the double-decker buses with open tops on Michigan Avenue, and sometimes the quaint streetcars provided us with a liberal education as to the sights and sounds of the big metropolis

On these walks, Father would dream out loud with his mindful meanderings. He would talk about the building he had planned for his business made of colored glass, taller than any other building in the world. He would say, "Who knows, maybe someday they will even land a small aircraft on top of my building." He would talk about his good friend Mr. Eddie Rickenbacker, and what a great pilot he was during World War I. He would freely express his dreams of tomorrow which were full of nice and wonderful surprises. He was looking forward to getting back on his feet with expectation of justice coming down the pipeline.

All of these wonderful memories would soon be cloaked in sadness, as we were swept into the bitter taste of financial deficit. The full impact of the Depression years was being felt by everyone.

CHAPTER 16

Reprieve Awaits

Struggling with our situation, Mother became wrapped up in her duties with getting us dressed and out of the hotel room each morning. It was tedious. Father needed the full benefit of privacy from four fidgety little ones, as he laboriously poured over piles of papers or letters, in deep concentration. He was in dire need of complete quiet while he was working.

Business friends and constituents would fill the room with their business conversations and cigarette smoke for hours. Mother nearly died not only from the smoke inhalation but from frustration caused by lack of privacy. A cluster of small children charging through a small living space can not only be a nuisance but downright infuriating. And getting us presentable was in of itself a scramble to instant insanity, with our hair needs and hair bows.

Mother, who was not strong since the birth of our new baby sister, now given the name Juanita, found it difficult to get her strength back due to the recent siege we encountered with scarlet fever. Father must have realized that she could not last too long before the pressures would overwhelm her. So, in order to prevent another breakdown, he decided to send Mother back to her hometown to visit with her family.

Now, Mother neglected keeping in touch with her parents for many years. She had other preoccupations. However, the thought of going home, to where she had spent her childhood, was a song in her ears.

Her better judgment told her that the sooner the better. She felt that our childhood charades might soon warrant Father exercising his prerogative and cause him to resort to spanking, in order to obtain peace and quiet.

Father quickly took us to the nearest Greyhound bus station across from the Loop. Boarding the big bus, we waved goodbye to Father from the back window. We kept our sights trained on his image as he disappeared in the distance. Father figured a trip down home could do a lot to boost Mother's morale. Father was hoping a visit with her family would bring back the rosy color in her cheeks and a smile on her lips.

Down home was a resource that hadn't been tapped as of yet and had great potential. Mother could not have been happier. I could see the sunshine in her face. She had no regrets about leaving the hotel room. She showed reservation, pondering what her family would think of her dropping out of the sky with four little children. There had been so much time elapsed between her connections. It was truly over ten years with many truths that had been secretly concealed. She had not shared any of her bitter disappointments or past grievances with anyone, least of all her parents.

Father felt the trip would do us all some good, and that we could meet our grandmother and our grandfather, who were

Indian. I was so anxious to meet my grandparents. I envisioned real Indians which I had only met in storybooks. We set upon our journey to Mount Erie, Illinois, on a Greyhound bus. Together we huddled at the bus window with great anticipation.

    I was a full age of seven, but the excitement of the new place found me peacefully pacifying myself with my thumb lodged in my mouth. I struck an ugly pose, as I wrapped my fingers around my nose and was soon in the land of dreams. It was not long before Mother swiped a slap alongside my head, "You're much too big for that," she said. "A big girl like you with your fist in your face!" she scolded. I did not want my mother to be ashamed of me, and I wasn't a baby anymore, but my thumb brought me such comfort. "Mount Erie, everyone out," the bus driver shouted. The trip was over so quickly. I must have fallen asleep. I missed the whole panoramic view.

    We gathered ourselves together and moved toward the door of the bus. We proceeded to exit, walking toward something that looked like a general store. Mother was plotting her next move as we examined everything with our eyes. There were barrels of pickles and savory sauerkraut, huge hunks of yellow cheddar cheese, and dried sausages secured at the ceiling, swinging to and fro. There was hardware, paper fans, straw hats, fly swatters and fly paper, hoses, shovels, rakes and a huge scale. Several men all dressed in straw hats, costumed in blue denim, were sitting around a table giggling and snorting. They were pushing around little red and black round discs on a black and red checked board. From time to time, they would spit and laugh with an explosive lunacy.

    I had never seen such characters in all my life. They were chewing on a strand of slippery weed that was dangling and twisting in their mouth. They could spit and talk at the same time. They talked a funny kind of talk like nothing I had ever heard before. *Maybe it was Indian talk,* I thought to myself. *Maybe these fellows were some kind of Indians.*

As I stood in awe of my new situation, I began to feel hunger pains in my stomach. A nice man wearing a white apron, standing behind a big wooden counter, handed us a soda cracker. I noticed Mother, who seemed to be studying her thoughts. She was pondering what her next maneuver would be.

It appeared as if no one was in a hurry to get out of the store. There were men with their feet propped up on the counter sleeping under their straw hats. I thought it was rude for them to put their feet on the table, but they didn't seem to care either way.

Sonny Boy lingered near the door, and I could see he was interested in the horses tied up out front. I decided I had better watch him because he could dart out and get himself in a heap of trouble.

Mother started conversing with several of the men near the back of the store, and in her soft tones she seemed to be inquiring about someone. I could not quite make out her words, as I wasn't a very good lip reader. It appeared as if Mother was getting along well with them, and it seemed like she knew them from before. Somehow, I felt Mother belonged here. As unexplainable as it was, I felt that my mother had reached a happy medium between the lousy circumstances in the city and the no-place-like-the-country situations.

After what seemed like an eternity, a strange wagon pulled up in front of the store. The man tied up his "team," as he called it. He complacently strolled in the door. "Hey there youngin'," he called to Sonny Boy, who had pressed his nose against the screen door. A few other horses were also tied to the hitching post outside. They were slapping flies on their backs angrily with their tails. I had never seen flies that big in my whole life. "Well, I'll be dag nabbed, if it ain't Minnie Graham," he hollered in an excited manner or greeting; I couldn't tell which. "Hey boys, it's the Graham girl. Whatcha doing in these here parts? Thought you'd done left us country boys for the big city fellers long ago. How's them city fellers treatin' ya anyhow?"

Mother exchanged a few answers to his fountain of questions. Then she asked the crucial question of the hour. "How's Joshua? Have you seen him lately?" Mother seemed concerned. Joshua was our uncle, and Mother always said he was her little crippled brother. In my mind I pictured anything but a grown man and thought that he might be just right to play with. "Josh is the same as always. He roams around the whole dern county, free as a breeze. That guy has got better sense than to get himself all married off to some girl who can't cook worth a woodpecker," the man went on and on. As I listened intently, the funny way he talked fascinated me. I had never heard this kind of conversation from anyone.

Mother lingered a while longer, and it appeared as if she was waiting for someone to offer a ride to Uncle Josh's place. The message finally got across to the old fellow named Hank, who was loading his wagon with supplies. He offered to assist. It sure took people out here a long time to get around to asking and doing things.

Hank hollered, "C'mon chillins, let's get the wheels a-rollin. Climb in. Bet ya ain't never seen a wagon like this before, now have ya?"

"No sir," we chimed. We climbed aboard while Mother was helped into the wooden plank seat stretched across the front. She sat baby Juanita in her lap. The baby peaked around to see where we were. I could see she wasn't too happy having to sit up front, but she was much too small for a rickety ride in the back of this old wooden affair.

Hank called out, "Do you know what I call my wagon?"

"No sir," I replied.

"Well now this dang antique is called a buckboard. Ever heard of a buckboard?" he asked.

"No sir," we responded.

As we settled down into the back of the wagon, he flicked the reins on his horses and we were thrown to one side. The long, laborious ride was a bit rough as we clopped down the deep ruts of what might be considered a common path, with its picturesque land of lush greenery. I thought that if Uncle Josh lived in this kind of place, that this must surely be the correct environment for Indians.

As the backwoods began to unfold, it became a carpet of green grass and culverts and roadside ditches. I began feeling as though I were in a jungle. I had never dreamed that Mother came from such a swell place.

I loved my mother dearly, but many times I felt that she did not fully understand me, not like Father did. Sometimes, she would victimize me with her banishment. This bothered me, but I was just now realizing that she was a vast reservoir of untapped common sense. She had sound judgment, as well as a wonderful wit. I wondered why my mother had not told us stories of her birthplace. To me, this seemed to be much better material for a good story instead of fairytales. My thoughts ran rampant. This was beyond my wildest dreams. At any moment I envisioned the possibility of a big tiger or lion creeping out from the bush. A lazy snake slithered across the wagon tracks, while a rabbit dashed madly for a thicket as we passed by.

The fields were blooming with every kind of weed imaginable. The flowers were wild and of every hue of the rainbow, some tall and some small. The roadside vegetation seemed to nod its head in welcome as the Snyders went on by. I was so tickled inside with exuberance that it showed. I struggled trying to reach the back of the wagon to dangle my legs over, but Mother turned to caution me against a possible accident. I longed to get down off the slow cumbersome wagon, as it labored over some mighty deep terrain.

As I looked behind me, Mother seemed to be rocking from side to side with baby Juanita in her lap. I knew Mother liked to rock, but this time the motion was in a different direction. It was a side to side rocking motion which looked uncomfortable. However, if you've ever watched a man who truly rides with his horse, then you can see how the two become as one. Mother knew the proper way to ride a buckboard. She just rolled with the tide of motion. It was hilarious watching Mother handle these maneuvers. We too were enjoying our anything-but-gentle ride. The buckboard was indeed the most exciting mode of travel bar none.

Now, I suppose one could have walked faster than the horse team clopped along and probably with a lot less dust being raised. With this thought crossing my mind, I thought I might attempt to do just that. I wanted to get out and run across the big open field and pick flowers, for everything looked free for the taking. But, I knew I better not try these daring antics just yet.

As Mother and old Hank conversed, I caught a faint glimmer of the baby turning a rather Indian red. She seemed to be afraid, but Mother was holding her securely, as she chatted like a magpie. Somehow, the poor baby seemed frightened. Maybe it was because she thought Mother might lose hold of her. It all seemed so funny to me.

If Father were only here he wouldn't believe it. There was Mother sitting up there bold as you please with a worried papoose in her lap, waving her arms in a tomahawk fashion. With her tongue in gear, she sure could chatter much more than I could comprehend. It was as though her tongue was loose at both ends. She was busy telling the old farmer, Hank, our whole life history. Hank seemed more than a little interested in Mother's story, and he had difficulty paying attention to keeping the horses on the path.

This land of the Indian was Mother's hometown, and I was glad to be here. As we rode along, the horses would flick their tails at the gigantic flies that rode on their backs. Those flies were enormous. It was an awesome sight. The old farmer laughed, "Ain't never seen one of those devils, have ya now?"

"No sir," I politely answered.

"Well now, thar a dang nuisance, and they will vex a mare to death iffin they've a mind to." These flies were nasty and buzzed and bit as they flew by. I decided I did not like them "devils," as he called them.

When the wagon pulled up for a stop in the middle of nowhere, I wondered if anyone lived around these parts. The houses were few and far between, way off in the distance. Using the Indian salute to shield my eyes, I squinted to support a satisfactory view.

As Mother was helped from the stiff, standard seat of the buckboard, we hopped off the rear section screaming with delight. With my nose full of fresh air and surrounded by beautiful flowers, tumbling out of the wagon, I jumped up and down in war hops of complete freedom.

The horses were breathing heavily, and the farmer seemed anxious to move on. Mother thanked the farmer and waved goodbye. I looked around for a house, but none was in sight. I wondered why Mother had chosen this lonely spot where obviously nothing could be seen except stretches of sassafras saplings. Mother sat the suitcase down and placed baby Juanita on top of it. She cautioned me to watch over her for a minute. Then she disappeared into the thicket.

If Uncle Joshua lived here, surely his home was hidden in the woods. After waiting several minutes, I struggled with the baby and the suitcase, as we followed Mother's path into the thicket.

We forged deeper into the edge of the brush and came upon a large clearing, large enough for a compound. Lo and behold, there was a little shack, a humble hut in a private wilderness. It was built out of strong, sturdy, straight logs and seemed quite strange, if not bewitching. The logs were unpainted and peeling, as if their skins were slipping from them. The little house was complete with a window and a door, but it was hardly big enough to accommodate a family. A nearby space revealed there had been a huge farmhouse at one time, but it was obvious that a fire had destroyed the structure many years prior.

After several minutes of continuous knocking, it was definitely decided that Uncle Josh was certainly not at home. Mother seemed puzzled and slightly confused, as she sat down on the top of the suitcase and began to ponder. Without an hourglass or a timepiece, it was impossible to tell just how long we were standing there. We were getting restless. Obviously we needed to wait for Mother's command. Mother was becoming more aware of our needs. Our toileting urges were never a problem, for Mother explained that no one was looking anyway. Our parching thirst needed to be quenched, and our monkeyshines did not deter our squabbling.

Mother tried to figure out a way to cope with our antics and began to explain that Uncle Josh built his home. That he liked to be alone and did not want to keep pace with the world at large. She told us how Uncle Josh was a dwarf and how he was crippled by a fall from a highchair when he was a small child, and this accident alienated him from social contacts. She said he liked his remote way of life in his secluded place.

Mother remarked, "Josh is my youngest brother and he never married. He has no ties, and he comes and goes as he wishes. He traps and hunts his food and lives off the land. When he gets lonesome, he goes from one farmhouse to the other and fixes radios. This is his life. He loves being a radio doctor."

I inquired, "What's a radio doctor?"

Mother replied, "Child, a radio doctor is a man who repairs radios. That's all I know. Josh has always tinkered with radios since he was young. He fixes all the neighbors radios."

By the time our conversation about Uncle Josh was dropped, Mother made a welcomed discovery. She rose from the suitcase where her backside left a funny imprint. Slowly the air sucked back in making shrill sounds, like bird calls, as the small hollow in the suitcase began to rise and straightened slowly. Mother had spotted a circular brick wall with a roof on top. It was a dollhouse-style looking house with a thick rope dangling from its center with an attached bucket.

"What's this?" Sonny Boy asked anxiously, as he tried to mount the brick wall in a jockey manner.

"It's a well. Now get down from there quickly," Mother scolded. "What do you want to do, fall in?" Mother then slowly untied the rope from the post and dropped the bucket down the well. I could see she was no expert at obtaining the liquid. She was having a difficult time sinking the bucket. After several unsuccessful tries, she finally managed to do so and then began to pull it up with all her might. As the bucket twisted its way to the top, she said, "I'm a little rusty," sort of under her breath. "I haven't sunk a bucket since I was a young girl."

Drawing a bucket of water seemed to be a struggle if not an intense chore. The rope pulled downward in resistance, as the water refused to remain in the confines of the bucket. When the bucket reached the top it was plain to see that most of the water had sloshed out, spilling back into the blackness of the endless pit. We would have to try again for a full container.

Mother called each of us in turn for a drink of cool, refreshing, crystal clear, well water. I looked down at the rim of the bucket; the water was pouring out between the slats of the seams. Mother commented, "Looks like Uncle Josh needs a new bucket." When I leaned down to position myself for a drink, I caught a glimmer of my distorted reflection in the ripples. As I took a sip from the bucket, water got in my nose. I nearly strangled. It was then that Mother showed us how to do it like real Indians. With hands cupped together, we dipped into the water to retrieve our refreshing samples up to meet our lips. It had a somewhat different flavor and seemed almost sweet instead of medicated. I was beginning to get the hang of this Indian life, and I liked what I saw. I thought to myself, *I'm going to have so much to tell Father when I see him. He won't get a word in edgewise.*

After we had our fill of water, we leisurely strolled back toward the road with our suitcase. Mother suggested we walk up the road a ways to see what was going on. I was beginning to get a mite worried, as we stalled and stumbled in contemplation. I could tell Mother was pondering her next move but had not yet made her decision.

Suddenly, we heard a sound from behind us and turned around to look. There, off in the distance, was a horse galloping toward us, pulling a funny black buggy. A woman, with a sun bonnet covering her head, had her arm stretched out using a switch to tap the horse's rump in a teasing manner. "Whoa, Whoa," she called loudly. The horse came to an abrupt stop.

Immediately, the strange woman saw Mother and recognized her. "Minnie Graham, what the dickens you doing out here in the sticks with all these kids?"

Mother seemed happy. "Why, Mrs. Price, it is so nice to see you again. It's been almost ten years, and I surely didn't think you'd know me the way I've changed."

"Girl," Mrs. Price went on, "you haven't changed that much. I'd recognize you anywhere. I suppose you just left Josh's place down the road. For heaven's sake girl, Joshua is never home. He's an old salt this time of year. He joined the Merchant Marines and takes off for places unknown. He stays on boats, some kind of cabin boy, I guess." Mrs. Price seemed to flow with a fountain of facts. She climbed down from her buggy and cautioned Sonny Boy and Velma to stay away from the mare, stating, "She's a mean old one around children. She's not used to kids, and she likes to kick."

As the two women moved toward each other, Mother put the suitcase down and started to converse.

"What happened to the home site? Did it burn down?" Mother questioned Mrs. Price.

"Well Minnie, evidently you didn't hear what happened. You know your pa passed away a couple years back and your ma stayed on a while. Then she took sick and just went so quickly. No one could do a thing to help. Then after they passed, something happened to the whole place; a fire I guess. Anyway, the barn and the main building just burned to the ground. Can't say much more, as people around here are so far apart that it's impossible to say what did happen." Mrs. Price just rattled on, as

Mother's face flushed a bit from the shock she was experiencing. She didn't smile. She seemed sadly serious.

"You know, Mrs. Price, I came here hoping that I could stay with the folks at home, but when I arrived in Mount Erie no one mentioned anything at the store about Josh being in the Merchant Marines or the fact that my folks were dead or even about the house burning." Mother seemed confused.

"I know, Minnie; sometimes it is best not to hit people with bad news. Or maybe, they thought you already knew about it, but whatever the reason there is nothing we can do about it here in the middle of this road. So, let's put that bag of yours in the back end of the buggy and pile them four kids of yours in somehow. We'll go to my place and get a decent bite to eat. I'm headed that way now. I'll just put an extra plate on the table. Don't worry your head about the details now. We'll figure something out between us. Come on, kids, pile in, and don't frighten the mare for she's marvelous at pulling the buggy but a pain in the neck when she gets upset or nervous."

As we piled into the cramped space of the buggy, with the baby on Mother's lap, Velma squeezed between the two women. Sonny Boy and I arranged ourselves between the ladies legs against the floorboards and seated ourselves in a stationary fashion. As we trotted along, the dust from the mare's hooves flew into my nostrils and coated my tongue with grit. The two women talked softly, and I drifted off into the silent world of my own thoughts. I wondered what Father was doing back in Chicago. I wondered if he was thinking of us and when I would see him again.

I could tell Mrs. Price and Mother liked each other for they busily chatted. They talked on and on, and before I knew it, we pulled into a clearing filled with several white buildings. Some were small, some were tall, but they were commonly grouped together like a friendly fortress. I thought to myself, *This is what a farm should look like*. It was a virtual oasis of civilization right in the middle of deserted prairie land.

I had not specifically paid attention to the news that Mother's parents were dead, and as of yet, I was still under the impression they were somewhere around. I wondered when I would meet my grandfather and my grandmother, the Indian ones. *Should I ask?*

As the buggy came to a commanding halt, Mrs. Price unhitched the pony and beckoned for us to make ourselves at home. I looked around and could see many lovely flowers in the front yard. Mrs. Price directed us, "You children can play on the swing out there under the tree, and soon I'll have a bite to eat for all of you."

Something to eat! What a welcome thought for sure.

I liked Mrs. Price. We had been hungry many times and learned never to ask, just be patient, especially when you are a guest. As we waited to be called, my siblings played contently on the swing. This was a totally different kind of swing than we had ever seen, not like in the parks. This one had two benches facing each other and a flat form in the center to stand on. While the others were ensconced upon the seats and seemed perfectly happy, I had things to think about. I was leisurely looking around at my new environment.

Soon, we were called in for our meal. I was jolted upon entering. The table was huge, much like the one at the restaurant, Henrici's, back in Chicago. It was bigger than our bed that we slept in, spaced like sardines all neat in a row. Her home was full of comfortable chairs covered with bright-colored material. There were fancy lace curtains on the windows. She even had a separate room with nothing but food in it. I knew instantly this lady wasn't as poor as we were.

She pointed to our places, and we took our seats in a mannerly fashion, for we were taught manners very early on. Mother never had to caution us about our etiquette. We learned to wait until we were served and tried never to spill or slop food.

Mrs. Price complemented Mother on our manners, and Mother beamed like a streetlight on Michigan Avenue. That night we ate and ate until we had more than we had ever had at one sitting. During the meal I listened intently as Mrs. Price and Mother conversed back and forth. "Too bad Joshua wasn't home, but then how could you know? It's mighty hard to keep in touch out here in the sticks. Even the mailman gets delayed and stuck in the ditch for a couple of days."

Mother inquired, "When's the last time Josh was in these parts?"

"Well, I don't rightly know. He's so dang-fired restless, always on the go. When he returns he heads straight up town to the barbershop where he tells his seagoing stories. Josh is a popular fellow around these hills. With people always needing to have a radio fixed, they can depend on Josh. I suppose he's out there floating around on one of those merchant ships right now. Probably like a whale taking in sunshine on his back. You know, I feel totally sick about your ma and pa. The kids never got a chance to meet their grandparents, now did they?" Mrs. Price was rambling on and on.

Mother's pale coloring flowed like starch into her skin as she spoke, "No I was hoping they would get to meet their grandparents. They don't remember their grandparents in Detroit either. My husband just lost his mother and his grandmother, and we just buried our little baby, June, in 1929; she died from membrane croup. It has just been one death after the other. Now, my folks are passed on too. I wasn't much for writing, and I kind of lost track. I never shared my troubles because I didn't want to worry them. When Cecil decided to send us down here, I was thinking how good it would be for all of us. Now this is another setback."

As I listened, I got the drift of the conversation, and I realized that "passed on" meant another grandmother and grandfather had bit the dust. I was cheated again, missed the boat.

For a moment Mrs. Price's information snatched Mother from reality, and I almost thought she would break down and cry. Indians are strange people, for Mother always tried to keep her feelings to herself. "I don't know where to go. Josh's place is hardly big enough for a good-sized doghouse," Mother was contemplating out loud.

Mrs. Price, recognizing Mother's plea, blurted out her idea, "Now, Minnie, you and I have been separated by miles and minutes, but our friendship is very close. I'd like to help. I've got that cute little house out there across the road. We haven't used it for living quarters for years, but the stove works in there. I could get it ready with your help. It would be ideal for you and the kids until something better comes up. Course there's about ten layers of chicken poop on that wooden floor. But, we can get to scraping, and before you know it you've got a place to stay." Mother had to depend on outside help and gratefully accepted the generosity of Mrs. Price.

After we finished our lovely dinner, with our bellies full of fried chicken, blackberry pie and country milk, we excused ourselves from the table to go play outside. Mother and Mrs. Price began to clear the table. I exited onto the porch, as their voices faded from earshot. The others ran for the swing.

Mother and Mrs. Price finished the dishes, while we ran off our dinner by chasing the chickens. It wasn't long before Mrs. Price noticed our little game that we were engaging in, and she got after us, telling us that if we frightened the chickens there wouldn't be any eggs for breakfast. I did not know how that applied, but I accepted her warning.

Several days later, the little house across the street was in order. We then settled in with our one suitcase and a few incidentals, which Mrs. Price gave to us. We had no need for a bed. We slept on straw pallets on the floor. The clean sweet-smelling hay was warm and dry like a feather bed tickling us all over. We were thankful to God and Mrs. Price.

When night fell, many times I would sit up with Mother on the steps just outside the door of our new home and take that opportunity to talk with her. I would ask Mother about the immense blackness of the night, for only the moon gave light to the surrounding darkness. Mother would assure, "There is nothing to be afraid of. It's not like the city with strangers who stalk at night. Here there are only little animals stirring around in the darkness looking for food." I could not see how any animal could find food in that darkness. This intense blackness seemed creepy and somehow dangerous.

When daylight streamed through the trees, Mother would get us up and send us over to the big house where Mrs. Price lived for fresh milk and eggs. We were enjoying this country life. Life was plentiful, and it agreed with us.

Then one day, a letter came in Mrs. Price's mailbox. It was from Father. He was announcing a new success and requesting our return to Chicago. Soon, we were saying goodbye to Mrs. Price, to our little house and our wide-open spaces. We were leaving without ever meeting Uncle Josh. He was still at sea. I had longed to see our uncle and our grandparents, the Indian ones, but the circumstances did not make it possible.

Reluctantly, we said goodbye to Mrs. Price and thanked her for her kindness. Mother promised to repay her as soon as Father's business got better, but Mrs. Price refused to think of any such thing. She seemed happy to have helped the family in a time of need. Our migratory return was soon initiated, as Father executed his command and Mother responded with her organizational talents.

We left Mount Erie by train this time. Mother said she preferred the train instead of the bus with such a bunch of kids, all with active kidneys and rambunctious energies. When our blowhole steam engine with attached boxcars arrived, Mother explained this train was a mail train and it hit every whistle stop. The train was fun and would become another diversion for our pastime. We were at last on our way back to life with Father in the big city.

CHAPTER 17

The Journey Back

Meanwhile, Father was breathing new life into his business, but the legislatures were huffing and puffing their bad breath at the nape of his neck. He had no fears, only a tremendous sense of personal security, which in itself was not contagious as far as Mother was concerned. Father was not evading responsibility; responsibility seemed to be evading him. The real clincher was the Depression.

Father knew full well that he was up against the psychotic government of politics, a government that made no simple miscalculations when armed to the teeth with intent to wipe out a man or an idea. Nonetheless, Father forged ahead, but the government was still not through practicing voodoo. They continuously stuck pins in Father's balloons of hope and expectations, as he sought justice from the states infringing on his patent and copyright.

The Secretary of State of Michigan, with a lack of responsibility, proclaimed no wrongdoing in public office, the underlined outcome of the court cases. This practice for the State Department to disavow themselves of any responsibility when wrongdoing is afoot is not new. The State Governments should be held responsible for crimes against inventors who suffer deprivation of their intellectual property under Sovereign Immunity infringement.

The Indian is not the only vanishing American. The spirit of the inventor, the ghost riders of the past and future, those who have been infringed upon by a Sovereign Entity, or will be in the future, will continue to give and give and never receive merits for their aspirations. Mankind has seldom acknowledged those who are not in front or center. My case in point, the Roman Empire was built anonymously, while far too much praise was given to an overrated Nero.

As for Mother, she saw things differently. She was fully aware of Father's ups and downs on the elevator of insecurity with his financial resources. Although these factors were far beyond Father's control, Mother was beginning to take on the aspects of a martyred wife. Prudish expediency on her part allowed her to be critical of Father's never-ending dilemmas concerning his forthright inventions. Father was himself and Mother was herself, and never the twain shall meet.

Upon settling back in at the hotel, Mother described our return as being anything but joyous, more like going to jail. Our happy reunion did not encompass any brass bands, nor did Father consent to signing any autographs. But he did kiss the baby, and things were fairly normal for a while.

Then unexpectedly, Father was confronted by the hotel management. He was in need of an extension on his credit. He pleaded in a manner of conviction that he would soon be caught up, but the hotel refused to grant any more credit. Father and Mother then retreated humbly, as they withdrew from the hotel living quarters. Without heated animosities being displayed, we relinquished some more of our meager belongings to the storage department for collateral security. It seemed like Mother died a little each time these things came about, but Father never outwardly showed too much concern for circumstance, especially when he was busy slaying dragons of the day.

He was as great with his diplomatic withdrawals as he was with his forward marches. He would turn in the keys at the front desk with his trusty umbrella over his arm. The hock shop already had his cane. He would proceed as if he were going out for a cup of coffee and would return shortly. In reality, he knew that he was virtually being evicted in no uncertain terms. He knew he was at the mercy of the almighty dollar. Exiting, he would graciously leave his forwarding address as "general delivery," which quite oddly enough would become his permanent address in later years.

Mother felt that, realistically speaking, things were far better off down on the farm than what Father had to offer. At least we had a roof over our heads and plenty to eat. Father, on the other hand, settled for the togetherness of the family with or without a roof. Prosperity was sure to be around the next corner. Only trouble was that when we reached the next proverbial corner there was no sign of prosperity.

Things were tough all over. Some people, including us, were worse off than before. But, Father had a seemingly endless supply of friends who were always there to retrieve him from the cliff of disaster. One such friend had a slew of housekeeping apartments for rent directly above the Ricketts Restaurant. It was within walking distance of the famous Lincoln Park and the fabulous Newberry Library. This delighted Mother, for we were getting bigger and required more space to "explode," as she put it.

Our new landlord was a kindly gentleman, about Father's age. He wore his hair smooth and sleek to the back of his head and carried a pair of horn-rimmed glasses positioned on his nose. Our very first meeting with him was a matter of routine introductions. He cautioned us with instructions as to what to do and what not to do in the building. Exercising his prerogative of a strict innkeeper, he warned us children about the dangers of the elevator on the opposite side of the building and about running through hallways and down stairwells. He advised us that we should stay away from the Ricketts Restaurant, located below us.

The landlord's rambling residence was a huge complex of kitchenettes, which in themselves were neat and well-kept. Out in front of this massive structure was a busy street corner with well-established bustling businesses. Streetcars clanged noisily to and fro. We were cautioned about darting into the street or from between parked cars. Being the oldest, I needed to look out for my younger brother and sister.

Meanwhile, Father was busy working on the reorganization of his business. He was still hemorrhaging from early wounds from mounting legal fees from failed court cases, but he was bound and determined not to let their political wizardry hinder his application of elbow grease to the problem at hand.

The pull of the people's interest had increased tremendously, but keeping the family in a proper dwelling while supplying Mother with bouquets of benefits, was a different matter.

When Father went to bed at night he didn't count sheep; he counted thieves.

It truly can be said he was busy bringing in the thieves. The mumble jumble of the politicians, with at first you see it and then you don't, was a clever convenience of corruption. Congress was either having a recess in the sandbox or playing games of monopoly. They were holding a trump card *in the deck of the future*, playing it years later, in 1938 to be exact, under the pretense of "Is he sane? Let's continue to drain game."

The magazine article from *Time* dated Monday, October 24, 1938, under the heading: "$20,000,000" stated, "In Chicago, Inventor Cecil L. Snyder, 45, told his wife Minnie that he had thought up a plan that was going to make him $20,000,000. Because they were on relief, Mrs. Snyder promptly asked acting County Judge Albert E. Isley to commit him to an institution. In court, the head of the Cook County's Psychopathic Hospital and his assistant both testified that Snyder was insane. Taking the case into his own hands, Snyder explained his plan (to sue twenty-eight states for infringement of a system he had invented for registering automobiles), and declared it would return $20 for each $10 invested, and asked for backers. After two hours of deliberation, the jury found Cecil Snyder *sane*." Snyder said with a knowing smile, "It was just a conspiracy to get control of the $20,000,000."

Father continued to face uncertainties because of his decision making. One such decision threw him into the limelight and not in a highly regarded way. In 1932, when the Lindbergh baby was kidnapped at the tender age of twenty months, the whole world rose up and cried for this dastardly crime. Colonel Lindbergh's uncle, John Lodge, was a business constituent and personal friend of Father's. Father immediately jumped on the bandwagon to help find the killers. It was indeed a horrible crime. Father would work as a handwriting expert on the case with the Chicago Police Department, but even this would not deter the negative portrayal of his good intentions.

On January 17, 1936, the *Chicago Herald and Examiner* newspaper had this heading, "Gangster Snyder Vital Element in Search," referencing him as "Petty Detroit Racketeer." *The Herald Chicago and Examiner* January 16, 1936, article titled: "Chicagoan's Amazing Tale Names Fisch," spewed columns, lined with print, describing Father's involvement with the kidnappers of the Lindbergh baby. Everywhere you turned, Father's name was projected in an unfavorable light.

It was apparent there was no reprieve for Father from media attention. There was no rest. He was constantly meeting with strange men who would come in and out of our small living quarters. Mother became really upset with prevailing conditions because of the kidnapping scare and the bad publicity Father was receiving. We could no longer be unsupervised or unattended for fear of ramifications. Mother would now accompany us everywhere we would go.

During one of our chaperoned outings, we passed the Newberry Library with its high spiked iron fence. Among the bushes, Sonny Boy, who was now adopting Junior for his identification because he was getting older, found a large brown portfolio. It was neatly tied with a little bow and contained a really large sum of cash, stocks and various other business papers of importance. Junior, who climbed over the fence to secure the brown envelope, handed it to Mother who opened it and examined the contents.

Inside was the identification of an address which was somewhere nearby and within walking distance. We proceeded to the street and number on the house and rang the doorbell. A large, well-dressed man opened the front door. Junior, who was a mere six years old, proudly presented the man with the particulars as to how he had come by the package. Without hesitation, the unsympathetic man snatched the portfolio from Junior's hands and muttered, "That's mine. What are you doing with it?" Junior, who was proud of his deed, was expecting a thank you and possibly a reward, which was obviously not forthcoming. Stunned by this man's reaction of ungratefulness, Junior ran down the steps of the stone building frightened out of his wits. The man just slammed the door in his face. Mother just shook her head in disbelief.

This unfortunate incident would leave a lasting impression and be a crucial turning point in Junior's life. He would remember how ungrateful some people are, especially the rich. It was quite evident that this man was a stockbroker with credentials that were incriminating to say the least.

At this stage of the game, Mother decided we definitely needed some religious instruction to guide us on the right path. We were then enrolled in Sunday school for religious involvement. It was marvelous training and a wonderful experience in fellowship and friends. We learned our Bible stories and faithfully memorized the verses and songs.

I soon felt the warmth and glow of this mysterious God and man, who was called Christ. The message that He first loved me made me feel good all over. The fervency with which I absorbed this religious instruction was further enhanced by my curiosity of others deep in prayer, as I innocently peeked into their lowered faces while they knelt nearby. With their eyes closed, I could see an undeniable light shining in their face, as they talked to God and knelt on the hard wooden floor of the little mission.

Never shall I forget the face of one lady, about forty years of age, praying with tears smeared down her cheeks. She clutched the back of my chair, and her lips moved in open prayer. My squinting vision and searching looks were rewarded in the wonderment of another's face. I wanted to know all about this wonderful God, who could make a light shine in someone's face.

Sunday school became a must, and we never missed prayer in the evenings. At the end of our Sunday school session, we would race home with the folded and colorful leaflets of our lesson of the day. I would read mine over and over to Mother. And when Father wasn't too busy, I would tell him all about Jesus. Father believed in God. He many times said that man receives most of his wisdom and knowledge by looking, observing, feeling, listening and by just keeping in touch with nature. However, I wasn't quite sure he knew about our new friend Jesus. I often sat on his lap and retold my Sunday school stories to him. Father always listened intently. I wanted to share my message. Father would hold me close, and I would whisper my truths in his ear.

Our Sunday school was uneventful, but our regular schooling became a problem, with our family's name splattered all over the front pages of the newspapers. It made choosing a proper school environment a dilemma. Father's position placed us in jeopardy. So, Mother sought secrecy, seclusion and security from the harsh publicity; she placed us in Catholic school. The nuns welcomed us with open arms, even though we were not Catholic. The nuns understood Mother's problem and guaranteed our seclusion in the Catholic school.

Each morning we attended mass in the huge cathedral. Our school nuns wore long black habits, which made them look towering and distant. I was respectful of their status with "Yes, Sister," which soon became my new household word. In my uniform of navy blue with my little red tie, I blended into the vastness of the big institution.

The lining up process became a part of my life, as did the daily masses in the darkened chapel filled with huge candles. The quiet solitude of the silent services, with the strange chants and responses, was very impressive and drew me inward toward the church. I knew little of the why and wherefores of this strange and fascinating way of religion. Many times, I knelt when I was supposed to sit and popped up only to find it was time to kneel. Embarrassed, I looked both ways only to find that no one bothered to look, and I felt at ease in the privacy I found.

While attending Catholic school during classroom study, the stern, strict nuns thought my left handedness was a display of defiance. They did not like my intestinal fortitude to remain steadfast. They would hit me with a ruler to try and "break my habit," as they called it. Trying to show them how well I could write with my left hand only created more suspicion of my so-called "attitude" toward learning properly. Father finally stepped in to rescue me from their wholesale abandonment. I was properly removed from the rank and file of the private school.

Since school choices were rather slim because of Father's situations and preoccupations, Mother would remain the judge and make decisions where I was concerned, at least for a while. Finally, when their minds were made up, I was enrolled into the public school system. By then I was so mixed up I could not concentrate, having been pulled in and out of schools so many times, I hardly knew which end was up.

With our different school dilemmas, our after-school situations were spent seeking the finer things in life which were free, since money was out of the question. This of course included Lincoln Park where many hours were spent near the Historical Society, under the watchful eye of good old Honest Abe. Lincoln Park was the poverty people's playground. With benches stationed all along the paths, there was a never-ending sea of people. There always seemed to be a man reading a newspaper or sleeping under one somewhere.

As a youngster, memories of the parks and the backstreet alleys of Chicago remained ever present in my mind. Danger was lurking everywhere. Chicago was notoriously famous for its crime and corruption back in the '30s. The filthy tavern barstools always had a warm seat waiting its turn. We passed these bars many times, and the reeking odor filled your nostrils with a foul stench.

The country was a much better environment than the city, and I was beginning to compare the two with a wide-eyed wonderment. Even the old man who swept the streets with his giant push broom lacked enthusiasm.

The signs of poverty were everywhere. Streets were filled with mountains of trash. Rubbish lay for years in the vacant lots, where the poor exercised their prerogatives. The children found excitement sorting through the pollution. Using discarded items of waste, they played Kick the Can or Catch, with whatever was available. King of the Pile was actually played on someone's garbage mound. It was Chicago, my town, the only town I knew, the town I grew up in, a town filled with banging, clanging and smelly stink.

When all else failed for fabricated fun, I took my sister and brother for a ride in the forbidden cage. As I pressed the button, the iron caged elevator rose up toward the top floor. I felt a surge of defiance and accomplishment trickle down my spine, like a cold shiver. I was daring and had investigated the whole adventure. I then enticed the two younger ones to follow.

A sudden, compulsive jerk announced the end of the line, and we opened the shaky iron doors. Directly in front of the elevator was a tiny window. We rushed over to peek out. As we peered down looking toward the street below, we were discovered by a nice lady who inquired about our intentions. She had a room near the elevator and her door was open. She invited us to come in. After a little coaxing, we entered her room. She introduced herself as Delilah and said she shared the room with Babe, who was not home.

Delilah was obviously lonesome. She was having a cup of extremely black coffee and playing cards by herself. It was the entertainment of the hour. Her coffee breath made my nostrils crinkle as she asked, "Where do you children belong?" She offered to tell our fortunes after learning that we lived in the building.

I had no idea what a fortune was, but it seemed thrilling. Hesitant to indulge ourselves, the nice lady assured us that it was "just for fun." Well, she gave me a reading of sorts. "Someday, you will be famous and do great things," she predicted. This I doubted very much for she was unaware of my past failures, and I was loaded with worry that she could see my past. "You like books, I see," she said. "Someday, you will travel to a different land. Ah yes! What's this? Looks like you are going to be an archaeologist."

"What's an archaeologist?" I inquired.

"Well," she wisely contemplated, "an archaeologist is a person who digs things up from the past and discovers treasures." To me this sounded right up my alley. I decided immediately that was exactly what I should be. I was a seeker all right, but as yet I was a bit behind in finding buried treasure. This prediction was favorable, and I accepted the challenge.

When she mentioned digging up old bones and artifacts buried years ago in biblical times, I was absolutely convinced that this was exactly what I had been waiting for all my life. She had successfully brainwashed me. I decided at once that my first task would be to dig up my baby sister, my grandfather, and a couple of grandmothers for good measure.

Our good attentive behavior and interest, along with Delilah's friendliness, consumed the time, and the clock ticked away our visit before we realized it was time to go. I knew we might worry Mother if we were out of sight too long. We made a hasty exit. This time, instead of taking the elevator, we descended by way of the winding staircase, which wound around the iron cage with its tails hanging underneath like 1,000 strands of black spaghetti. These were thick cables used to anchor the elevator. I cautioned the others not to tell where we had been or what we had been up to. I felt safe they would keep our secret.

It was many days later before we ventured back near the hallway where the elevator stood faithfully waiting for a passenger. As we stood innocently by the door observing, someone on an upper floor had pushed the button and the elevator was called to duty. We watched with interest as the shaky cage mounted with creaks and groans to the floor above, hoping that the retrieved passenger might be our new friend, who lived on the top floor. As we waited with anticipation, the lowering cage suddenly became stuck between the upper floor and the lower floor.

A frantic call for help came echoing from above. We peered upward toward the ceiling where we could plainly see a man's feet and pant cuffs. He called down to us, and we responded by assuring the poor fellow that we were directly on the way for help. It wasn't long before the extremely perturbed man was released from the blasted thing.

It was a frightful reminder that our forbidden trip several days prior could have culminated in this exact sort of wretched event. We had missed a heap of unknown trouble and were reluctant to ever mount this cage again. I was responsible for Velma and Junior, and I warned them to never return without me.

In the evenings, we spent our time in the quiet shadow of Mother's rocking chair where we sat cross-legged and recited our Bible verses. As a witness for our Lord and Savior Jesus Christ, the first verse I learned was John 3:16, "For God so loved the world that He gave His only begotten Son, that whosoever believeth in Him should not perish, but have everlasting life." Many times, I thought the floor would swallow me up as I stood among the church congregation making my testimony for the Lord. With my knees knocking, I knew that I would never make a public speaker.

I was only nine, and each day that I got older only reminded me of the personal wonderment of being more involved with life and new exciting things. I was rather mixed up about many facts of life. I was only aware of the many things that I obviously had no common knowledge of other than what I overheard grownups talking about. I was an inquisitive child full of questions. I was seeking but finding no answers. I was attracted to keyholes of privacy or listening after dark to soft conversations. I sought answers from my mother, but she would passively resist answering them. She would tell me I was nosy, which hurt my feelings beyond repair.

Months passed, and the many newspaper articles about the Lindbergh's story and the gossip from the press releases about Father, caused Mother to crusade for care and comfort. Father's bad publicity was overwhelmingly abundant, but Father felt he should still help Colonel Lindbergh's uncle because he was a dear friend and Father was concerned for his plight. This is why Father put his efforts into full-time employment, joining with the forces for this investigation, acting as a handwriting expert on the case. His deep concern for other people caused him to totally disregard any warnings from family and close associates to steer clear of being involved with the Lindbergh case. Many, including Mother, felt he should direct his loyalties toward the people who backed and supported him with his business; but Father was a man of conviction and hard to convince. He was exactly that stubborn bull head that Mother spoke of.

As time passed, Father's lack of attention to his business was creating difficulty in answering to those who were in support of him. Their kinship of cooperation was wearing thin. Father was running out of steam in this fight for justice with the legislature, as the stink of the Depression was raining down on everyone. All was becoming a lost cause.

Mother felt it was unbearable to keep living this way because of Father's involvements. She was desperate. Father finally decided to appease her and plan another trip back to her hometown. He hoped to boost her morale. The necessary arrangements were made. Our belongings were gathered and loaded into the back of a battered old pickup truck, belonging to a friendly black family-man named Bill. With baby Juanita nestled comfortably in Mother's lap, we were whisked away to what Mother referred to as a better environment, while Father continued his struggles in the city.

CHAPTER 18

On The Road Again

Our 350-mile jaunt back to an earlier scene of triumph was typical, even though a nagging fear lingered that Bill's old truck might not make it. Mother rode inside the truck with Juanita. We weathered the trip outside in the back end of the pick-up truck, reclining on our backs, looking up at the sky. We were relaxed and enjoying a thrill of a lifetime looking forward to more promising events.

Arriving back at Mother's hometown in Mount Erie, we pulled over to rest a moment on the side of the road. We must have looked like oddballs—one black man, one Indian squaw, and four paleface papooses. An old farmer in a pair of bib overalls and a wrinkled shirt faded from the sun, moseyed over and approached the driver of our little caravan. He leaned against the side of the running board and straddled the tiny window with his arm. Calmly picking his teeth, he spit to the side of the road as he carried on farm dialogue seeped with southern drawl.

Our driver Bill explained our mission to the farmer and where we were headed. They seemed to get along well together. "Say, feller, how's that dang Depression up thar in Chee-ca-go' fectin' people? I heard tell the gangsters are running wild and takin' over the dang place. Zat so?"

The old black man slowly smiled and replied, "Don't believe evathang yo all hear cuz it haint rightly so. But, eny time yo all wants to take a trip up to see fer yourself, c'mon ahead. It's a mitey big place; yo all boun' to run inta crooks now 'n' then. Ain't no jobs nohow fer a feller. Better yo all fin' sompin' fer yoself rite down here." The old farmer got his fill of conversation and spit toward the ditch. "Guess yo all got to get goin'. A feller's better off in his own neck o' the woods," and he went on his way.

We pulled on down the road and began searching for Uncle Josh's secluded home. After missing a few vital turns here and there and backing up near a ditch and nearly getting stuck in a gully, we did manage to find the spot. We quickly unloaded our bits and pieces of personal stuff on the roadside. Uncle Josh was once again not home, and old Bill seemed concerned for our situation. He was convinced there might be no one forthcoming anytime soon. However, he indicated he could no longer linger with us and bid us farewell. As he pulled away, Mother cautioned him about making any wrong turns in the road and getting lost.

This was the second time we had come and still there was not a soul in sight. However, this sequel seemed more serious. We were destined to spend the night on the turf as twilight fell.

Meanwhile, we sipped from the well and cried uncle at the door. Mother sat once more on her trusty toadstool suitcase pondering if we should go in through the window, but Josh's window would not unlock. The weather was warm, and Mother laid down a spread on the grassy bank near the roadside. From sheer exhaustion, we were soon winking, blinking, and nodding off, dead to the world.

The postman came by early. The sound of conversation awoke me from my sleep. As I rubbed the cobwebs from my peepers, I heard the mail carrier speak some encouraging news, saying he would go down the line and send some help around. "Heavens be thanked," Mother sighed.

After the postman left, we quickly woke the others and splashed fresh, cool water on our faces and swished the sweet, pure well water through our lips to cleanse our ugly breath. There were only natural necessities —water, air, and a few berries for breakfast.

With the hope of help soon on the way, we babbled like brooks, as Mother seemed to come refreshingly alive. She had been extremely receptive to the heartfelt greeting of her fellow townspeople when we pulled into the square. Many must have known of our plight but could not help since they too were in despair. We weren't looking for a handout, for Mother had some money to pay rent and buy essentials. Mrs. Price was not aware of our second appearance from Chicago. Mother vowed we were not going to impose on her hospitality this time. We would be staying an unknown number of days, and Mrs. Price had done more than her share already.

Sitting on the uncut grass, Mother pondered our situation. It wasn't too long before help began to arrive. Seemed the mail carrier helped spread the word. A friendly farmer, named Sam Keyser, heard through the grapevine of our plight and pulled up in his cantankerous little Model T. He hopped out and began to load our things on the roof and proceeded to tie them down. We climbed in and placed a few things beside us on the seats. As we drove away, I looked back at Uncle Josh's cabin, as it slowly faded from sight.

Little did we know that Mr. Keyser and his family would become a vital link in the chain of events taking place in our lives.

CHAPTER 19

The Keysers

Pulling into the Keysers' Garden of Eden, Mr. Keyser gave us a complete tour of his complex working farm. The Keysers farmed on a large scale and had much land at their disposal. Their hard work blessed them with a substantial herd of cattle, a plentiful supply of sows, several varieties of chickens, mules and horses. All of this was guarded by their faithful shepherd dog, old Rover, who was strictly a working dog.

Nell was his good and faithful wife. She was a good mother and all-around hard worker. She kept a trim garden of produce, a large chicken and egg project and was skilled with milking, quilting, baking and cooking for the hired hands.

The Keysers were the kind of folks that shared their place with any orphans of a storm. They were well known for helping and were comfortable in their surroundings. Their table did not show poverty, which was prevalent in the city. They had tremendous responsibilities with their family of seven. They had five children,

Willis, Wilma, Wanda, Wallace, and Walter Lee. Of the five "W's," Willis was the oldest, and Walter Lee was the baby.

Their vast spread had several pieces of property in which stood vacant houses eagerly waiting for tenants. Mr. Keyser offered one of the little frame houses for our usage. Mother was delighted. She was instantly sold on green pastures.

Upon a complete inspection of the property, Mr. Keyser seemed to be in a particularly jovial mood. He would turn and spit the juice from his tobacco wad he was chewing saying, "I'm mighty surprised to see this old place still standing up by itself, but if you people can afford five dollars a month, it's yours. Course if you run short, we can just overlook that too. We don't rightly use this place anymore. The wife and I would love to have someone in it just to take care of it. It doesn't leak, and the windows all work. It could serve you right nicely." Mr. Keyser was speaking directly to my mother. With tears in her eyes, Mother looked straight at Mr. Keyser as they streamed down her face and said, "Mr. Keyser, I don't know how to thank you. I'll never be able to give you full measure in return, but this place looks wonderful. I would love to live here. I will clean it up a bit, and I'm sure I can get five dollars a month from my husband. It will be well worth the money. Besides, if you could only see how we had been living, you wouldn't believe it."

Except for a cook stove, which burned a combination of wood and coal oil, the place was virtually empty of any furniture. Necessity-wise, we needed only a table and a sofa, which Mr. Keyser offered from his own belongings. He promised to scrape together a few other things for us at a later date. There was no doubt in our minds; this house was the best ever. We gratefully thanked him for this refuge from the poverty prevailing back in Chicago.

THE KEYSERS

In reality, this was a fine old simple structure. It had an upper and lower floor. It was quite large with enough room for our little tribe. We paid our first month's rent to Mr. Keyser, who generously added a milking cow named Rose, along with feed for the cow from his corn cribs. Now, old Rose was a friendly, sociable cow. Her crusts of cream were so sweet and thick that she was soon to be our prize blue ribbon butter and cheese supplier of all time. These extras that Mr. Keyser supplied were more than enough in themselves and well worth the rent.

Later, Mr. Keyser had his two older boys, Willis and Wallace, come plow a tiny plot for Mother to have a small produce garden. Mrs. Keyser donated some chickens and ducks, and we acquired a cat and a small dog named Tootsie. It was a surefire answer to another world for all of us, and we soon felt right at home.

After settling in, we kicked off our half-soled shoes and proceeded to run through the open fields. This would become a normal joy of life, but not at the present. The clods of dirt were as sharp as shiny black stones under our tender feet. This greatly amused the Keysers who seldom wore shoes except on Sundays, to the little brick church.

Cecil Junior couldn't wait to climb into his first haystack with the younger Keyser boy, who was the same age. Wallace, sometimes affectionately called Wad, was the runt of the family, but he could do a full day of work like a man. Junior and Wad became the best of friends. They were two of a kind when it came to mischief.

Wad and his older brother, Willis, helped their dad with all the farming and could plow a field as neatly as the next fellow. Wilma, the oldest girl, did most of the baking for the family while Wanda, the middle girl, did a variety of chores. She would make beds, gather eggs, pick blackberries and carry water to the men in the fields.

Wanda became my dear friend, as well as my sister Velma's. She was our constant companion and confidante. Many times, she chaperoned us on guided ventures of country origin. We learned a variety of facts and lessons of life from Wanda. She would accompany us to the creek to swim and guarded us from the water moccasins. She knew where the biggest and sweetest berry patches were, and she taught us how to get an egg away from an old setting hen without getting attacked. Together we made mud pies and decorated them with green berries from the mulberry tree near their garage.

Little Walter Lee and little Juanita fell into our capable hands, as Wilma, the older girl, was preoccupied with thoughts of marriage. Her interests lay with one of the most eligible fellows in town. His name was Denny, and he had a fast "mow-sheen." When Denny called on Wilma, he not only raised a trail of dust clouds which hovered for hours before settling, but he left a few scattered and squished de-feathered chickens along the wayside. Wilma took many a ribbing during her courtin' days, as far as we youngsters were concerned. We watched and giggled and spied on these young lovers. We were the "CIA," (Children Interested Anonymously), as we displayed our shenanigans stemming from our peeking and booing policies. We would peek from behind the porch swing, behind the garage doors, which would be slightly ajar, or from almost anywhere, whenever Denny came a-calling on Wilma.

Our other activities of interest included enjoying fresh air and wide-open spaces. All day long, we were in motion. We ran our legs off. On one particular day, as the sun was beginning to set on the top of the ridge to the west, a race across the green pastured field was initiated. I took off running, pacing myself against the battling breeze with my mouth wide open. As I was running, a very courageous grasshopper hopped down my throat. I found his passing to be rather difficult. It was my very first encounter with the small green insect, and it was one not soon forgotten. His scratchy entrance into my esophagus led him down a one-way passage. I'm sorry to say, the grasshopper's predicament initiated violent vomiting. My already weak stomach chickened out on me, and I found my condition worsened to the stage where I needed to put my palate in pain. I was hoping to regurgitate this poor creature. Mother's words rang in my ears, "Maybe that will help you keep your mouth closed." She was right, for the risky rascal was beyond regurgitation. I suppose it looked hilarious to everyone, but to me this was no laughing matter. I could think of no legitimate reason or claim why anyone should have to enjoy the entrée of grasshopper, so please no encores.

With each passing day, our new country life brought new adventures. We learned the country ways, like one stayed at home when a road was impassable and tended to particulars at arm's length; and when roads were passable, one partook of the opportunity to venture in the other fellow's direction. Living was slow and sweet.

We learned to respect the animals and treat them with tenderness. When old Rose had her cute calf, we spent hours in the tiny pen grooming her for her mother, whose long tongue licked her little baby each day. She was a gentle mother cow and shared her baby with the family. It was only a stone's throw away from our front door that we witnessed Rose's calf being born. Mother had second thoughts about our seeing this miracle of life, but the matter came up so quickly that it was too late to rescind the decision. It made me rather sick at first, but I soon got over the incident.

Cows were valuable animals to a farmer, for most farmers did not butcher their cows. Beef was a rarity, and since milk didn't come from the same place the calf was born from, I had no qualms with nature. However, pigs wallowing in mud and slop left me little desire in my mind or appetite for ham or chops. The egg was quite another matter, a provocative phenomenon I pondered often. Mother was right; I was a finicky eater. I now knew why.

It must have been at this point in my life that I made a life-changing decision leaning toward vegetarian eating. However, my little sister, Juanita, had a very different palate. With her voracious appetite, she digested "specials" of fuzzy butterflies and fully intact caterpillars. While Mother was busy hoeing her garden, preoccupied with her endeavors, Juanita would linger near the lettuce looking for these hairy wormlike insects. She would pursue these tasty tidbits as an afternoon delicacy. Her strange tastes were an attempt to test her taste buds. Mother would scold, "No! No! We don't eat caterpillars," but little Juanita would persist in her mashing efforts to get the struggling critter in her mouth. "Guess maybe she's lacking something in her system," Mother would conclude. We never really ever found out what nutritional value the caterpillar supplied, but it was a relief to know Juanita acquired no further fuzzy tastes.

If this wasn't enough, little Juanita had temper tantrums two or three times a day. She would hold her breath until she turned blue. Ordinarily a dash in the cold water pail would bring her around, but sometimes even a face in a pail was without results. After passing beyond blue to the second dimension, she became milky white.

It was fairly obvious Mother had her hands full, and there was never a dull day. We were always discovering some new delight or provoking some new participation. We found lots of things to explore from early in the morning until late in the day.

When night fell, it was usually dark and quiet with the exception of one regrettable occasion. As we were mounting the stairwell for bed, in our usual manner, I took the lead up the darkened flight of stairs into this boogie blackness. Gripped in my hand, I was carrying water in a beveled sharp metal pitcher. I reached the top of the stairs, and to this very day I don't remember how it all happened, but my cowardly way caused me to catch the shadow of the kerosene light which danced on the smoked ham hanging from the ceiling. This grotesque image caused me to overreact, and I whirled around just as I reached the top of the stairs and lost my balance. I thrust the metal pitcher forward. It wound up going directly into the face of my baby sister. I fell into my sister, Velma, who was behind me carrying Juanita in her arms.

Because it was very late, we were left stranded. We spent the rest of the night hovering over her almost lifeless body. We had to wait till morning when Mr. Keyser could transport us in his Model T to his family doctor in town. Juanita's eye was badly cut, but fortunately for her I missed blinding her for life. Mother would interject, "Why don't you be more careful, Eleanor? Why don't you watch your sister better?" These were all reminders in my walk of shame.

With this primitive lifestyle, it was fairly obvious, mishaps were concerning. One did not necessarily need electricity and running water, but wall-to-wall surprises were inexcusable. Even the surprises contained in the old outhouse were not too bad after you got accustomed to the spiders and cobwebs. One dreaded a visit to this necessity of invention. With toilet facilities, out here in the country, being rather diversified and sometimes completely lacking, not many had the comfort of using catalog pages to wipe with. Most country folk used corncobs, which was no instrument of joy.

Getting used to this country life gave us lots of opportunities to explore even the simplest things. For example, using a big toe to penetrate a handy crusty cow pile was intriguing, if one took time to properly investigate it with their dusty foot. Now, crusty cow piles were neat, but chicken manure was more troublesome. Mother would look down the end of her nose when we tracked in this mean mess onto her freshly scrubbed wood floors. To minimize this dilemma, she placed a washbasin at the entrance of the door to wash our feet before entering. This was a requirement.

We also had other requirements, like chores. It was very important to pitch in and do our right and reasonable share. I loved to feed the chickens and soon learned the proper clucking sounds one has to make with the mouth to get the chickens interested in something besides the rooster. It is popularly known as "dumb clucking," a ritual, if not an incantation, which attracts one and all.

Junior, our little outdoors man, liked milking the cow, and Mother showed him the tricks of the trade with the correct procedure for pulling for gain. Soon, he became an udder expert. With manly pride, he was able to aim a parachuting stream right into the cat's mouth and never hit her between the eyes. Guilty many times of missing the milk pail, Mother would have to take over his knuckle-bearing antics; otherwise we would have a short supply.

THE KEYSERS

Cecil Jr. milking Rose, Velma wearing hat, baby Juanita

Mother was an expert with cow milking. She learned it before we were ever born. I perceived it as an old Indian specialty. With the bucket positioned between the cow's teats, she used the two-fisted system to pull the milk down. It was exceedingly funny.

Velma was our expert butter churner. She could shake down a Mason jar like a real pro, turning the butter flake mix into one creamy lump of pure sweet country butter. Being the strong-armed butter babe that she was, she had mastered a skill that later in life could be used to make a mean martini.

Another chore was wash day. Mother would rise early and put the kettle on for boiling water. A small campfire would be conveniently lit under the boiling oval tub which was quite popular in the '30s and '40s. Everyone boiled their clothes and stirred the batch with an ordinary broom handle. It was a witching job. It was difficult to tell whether the lady of the house was stirring a batch of chowder or boiling a bunch of clothes or even making soap. The technique was all the same.

The boiler had to be securely locked over the fire. It was a tricky maneuver. After the clothes bubbled for what seemed like hours they would be removed by the broom handle and a mighty strong pair of arms. Clothes would need to be lifted and carried over and dropped in a galvanized tub, which was also the same tub we used to bathe in once a week. Then the real work began. Mother would laboriously linger over the wooden washboard and rub until her knuckles were red.

On wash day, everything we owned went into the water. It took us all day to put the clothes through the ringing process. Manual dexterity and downright gymnastics is what it took to twist and tug and twirl the garment, squeezing out the moisture. It was no game for Mother, and she never complained. However, she did many times comment on how deeply we had penetrated the soil. Mother would use the words "yikes a mundo," possible Indian slang for the stains and spots that would not come out.

These days would become routine. We were happy and healthy living this country life. The vigorous health program provided by Mother Nature, and our fresh air school, was beginning to take effect. Our skin tones were changing from puny palefaces into inflamed Indians. Our skin had been kissed by the sun. Father would not have known us if he saw us.

With all this activity, our appetites were like filling stations. We were always stopping in for a final fill-up. Mother had very little chance to prove her culinary skills in the city, for she had almost nothing to work with. Many times she had said, "I'm tired of eating out of the can." As for me, I thought most food came from a can. Our living lessons learned in the garden provided, without a doubt, the knowledge that the best food came from the ground to the kitchen. Dandelion greens in a pot sprinkled with bacon bits and vinegar were pretty tasty. And digging taters, shucking corn, plucking peas and snap beans, even pulling carrots up from the ground was music to the ears.

We seldom saw a piece of commercial candy, and only once in a while were we treated to homemade fudge. Mother's fudge was made with hands of skill, and her samples were a delight.

Occasionally, the Keysers had a taffy pull. Ordinarily, one did not waste sugar for such luxuries. Wild nuts and sweet berries on the bush supplied enough treats for everyone.

Peach or blackberry cobbler was Mother's specialty. She would bake on Saturdays, in the morning, and leave it set until it became cool for cutting. Tomatoes were fruit, and vegetables went into most everything from soup to salad and were our in-between snacks. When we tired of milk, we switched to sassafras tea, which Mother prepared in the soup kettle and served to us by way of the big dipper. Lots of fruits and vegetables kept us regular, and the sassafras tea was for purifying the blood. We indulged very little with meat, and what we had was mostly chicken, ham or rabbit, and once in a while a quail.

Beside food for the body, Mother saw to it that we also had food for the soul. We loved going to church on Sunday morning. It was almost like the Clark Street missions with the preachers waving their arms and getting all red in the face. There was only one church for miles and everyone came. Wilma Keyser played the organ. Mrs. Keyser could be heard above the whole congregation with her high-pitched voice, as she rendered a good, strong version of that "Old Time Religion". She was the greatest.

The preacher man, as he was called, depended on the members of the congregation for his Sunday dinner. In fact, that was a fair exchange for a real ranting revival-type sermon. Sometimes, the industrious ladies league would make corn chowder for the congregation and the preacher man as well. The faithful of the church would bring their pails and buckets to the church service to fill and take a sample back home.

Evening prayer sermons were interesting. The ladies all sported fans of some sort or the other. It was fun to watch their different techniques with the fanning sessions. Some fanned leisurely. Some fanned lazily. Some fanned vigorously. Some fanned and fanned and missed, while others seemed to be fanning the person in the next aisle. All the ladies were devout fanners. Most of the time, I thought they must be using the fans as weapons of protection from the nasty flying moths swooping and dive-bombing the backs of innocent brothers and sisters bent in prayer. The flying insects were a menace for me. I hated the evenings when I had to sit and dodge them as they aimed and landed on my nose or neck. I had all I could do to stay properly seated. As the message came loud and clear from the pulpit, the louder the sermon got, the faster the ladies fanned to either stir up the miserable moths or cool off the flaming fires of hell.

During these sermons, one dare not leave before it was over, or all heads would turn in unison with hellfire and damnation looks. Unless one had a dire need to relieve oneself, you needed to sit quietly until the end.

To avoid heads turning, Mr. Keyser who knew that chewing tobacco was forbidden in the church, would position himself close to the back door. Mr. Keyser enjoyed a chaw of tobacco and could hold a wad in his mouth without ever being discovered. But many times, I saw Mr. Keyser slip out the door for a quick spit only to be followed by the watchful eye of Nell, his wife. I could tell Sam Keyser enjoyed his wad, for he could spit a proper length through the front of his teeth and aim quite a respectable distance.

While listening to the sermons, the cool moonlit evenings beckoned beyond the broad door of the church. The churchyard was filled with horses tied to trees and an occasional Model T car.

Our experiences with religion seemed to be successful, so Mother decided that we must build on our already good foundation. We must be saved. This expression brought fear, for I was unsure of the consequences. The annual baptizing was always done in decent weather, and I was soon to learn why. When Mother decided to have me saved, I had no idea what I was in for. Looking back, I could see I had not understood all of the sermons, for baptisms were mighty advocated. When I saw the other poor participants ahead of me getting a sound dunking from the preacher, I froze with fear. My nose was particularly sensitive. I knew I would strangle if I got water in my nose. I hung back wishing to stay inconspicuous at the rear of the line, hoping that somehow they might forget my turn, but no such luck. I was given a clean white handkerchief much like the ones Father used. As I listened to the singing voices behind me, I decided that I needed some saving from this here preacher man. A preacher looks one way in the pulpit, but out here in the middle of the river, he looked sinister, all dressed in black.

"Come forward, little lady," he said. I looked him square in the eye and could clearly see he was enjoying what he was doing. That twinkle in his eye was not inviting but seemed forbidding. I suddenly became afraid. I wanted to turn back, but the water was almost up to my chest. I had no alternative. I was about to be saved. I wondered what Father would say about all this.

I tell you, I nearly lost the faith that day. It was all over in a second. And it was my luck that the preacher nearly lost his balance, for I threw myself backward with such great force that I nearly took the preacher man with me. I came up strangling because water got into my nose. I struggled to get my balance. My hair was strewn all over my face, and I couldn't push it back. I dropped the handkerchief in the water and instantly realized I needed to be saved from the river. I had never learned to hold my breath properly, and I received a good sound dousing. I think I surprised the preacher man more than he surprised me. Embarrassed, I made a fast getaway.

As I sat on the riverbank ledge, wet and cold, I saw a reflection of my face in the ripples of the water. I began to stir the water with my great big trained ballet toe. As I leaned forward to get a closer view, I could see the distortion of my reflection. It was the same as when I viewed my reflection in the shiny rim of the brass spittoons at Father's office. It had been years, but it was apparent nothing had changed. I had not improved. I was nine and never viewed myself in a proper manner, because nothing was available to me to view myself. Opportunities to see your reflection only came as a surprise in some puddle of water, a doorknob of brass or a bright shiny spittoon.

As I continued sitting there reflecting, I could see the crowd was starting to break up and get ready to leave for home. I would remember this day even if I lived to be a hundred. My assurance was I now was saved. I thought, *I must tell Father all about this when I see him.*

Mrs. Keyser had tears in her eyes when she came up to meet me, and I suspected she was crying for my near drowning. My wet clothes were drying, but my clothes looked crumpled and uncomfortable. All in all, I managed to survive. Junior and Velma seemed to enjoy their dunking, but then they were too young to worry about incidentals.

The ritual and ceremonies that grown people participated in were ridiculous. I was dizzy from ruminating about them. Life was a puzzle to me and each piece needed to fit in with the rest, but sometimes the pieces did not want to fit where they were supposed to go.

I had all I could do to get a proper perspective analyzing each new thing so I could accept them. I would ponder researching in my mind, the good and bad of a situation, and by the time I finished my research the essence was lost, and the idea was no longer redeemable. I sometimes envied my sister. She always went headlong into situations seemingly without worry and showed no regard for consequence. Being born with an inquisitive mind, a questioning tongue and an analytical attitude, I seemed to rattle old bones. I wasn't always one who accepted things as they were, but I never ceased to remain firm on my foundation of rock bottom religion. As the waves of life spilled over me, the waters of time washed my sins away, and I became clean.

The following days were delightful. The dandelion seeds were drying in the sun spreading their seed pods into the atmosphere. The confirmation of the fall season was being displayed upon the harvest. The corn in the field ripened, and the shucks dried stiff on their stocks revealing the secret watermelon patches that Mr. Keyser had hidden, tucked here and there, throughout the fields. Our first venture into the watermelon patch caught me off guard. As I strolled through the corn furrows, I spied an evil charmer with a pair of snake eyes. I was unschooled in the art of snake charming, and I had no rabbit's foot to guard me. I knew this was no garden snake. I certainly wasn't about to ask for credentials. This devil was coiled and ready to spring. His eyes were locked and loaded and ready to face off with me. I sprung through the air with my feet frantically flying without any foundation, refusing to let this rattled renegade catch me. I left behind no carbon footprints.

Picking watermelons could certainly make your heart race, but true excitement came on Saturdays when Mr. Keyser would take us to town in his friendly fresh air winter buggy. He would load it up with cream and eggs to trade in exchange for weekly supplies. While there, we would be treated to the town's silent screen movie selection of the week. It was an outdoor affair. The projector flashed brown-toned serials on the outside wall of the general store. The audience remained in their buckboards, on horseback, or they would stand on the running boards of a Model T.

We would receive a piece of licorice or chewing gum for a snack during the feature. There was no sound, and the scenes were mostly westerns. After the trading was done, the women would exchange gossip or finish purchasing a piece of material for dressmaking. The men would hang around the barber pole disputing, reminiscing, hashing and rehashing events. When all necessities were gathered, we proceeded with our trip home.

These Saturday night outings would extend beyond the ten o'clock timeframe, which was considered an indecent hour and way past a respectable residence bedtime. Mother, who did not accompany us on these outings, for Juanita was way too young, never worried about us. She trusted Mr. Keyser implicitly.

Sometimes on our way back home, Mr. Keyser's winter buggy would stop short. It was a tiring task to prime the pump. Mr. Keyser would crank and chew, and chew and crank, showing frustration when he couldn't get the vehicle moving. He would spit a stream from his wad in his mouth through his two front teeth, and if the wind was in the right direction it would be a challenging maneuver to duck the propelled sprinkles.

Pounding his fist upon the brilliantly dull finish of the charcoal chariot did little but knock off the radiator cap. Never once raising his voice in curse, he would mumble under his breath, "This buggy needs a good swift kick." Many a time, we would have to push the buggy when it refused to go up small inclines. Very unpredictable, the dim-looking beams would strain to illuminate the bumpy, deep ruts in the road. It took two hands firmly grasped on the wheel so that you wouldn't miss the guidelines for maneuvers, otherwise you'd find yourself in a culvert or in a ditch. When this darn machine was acting up, we would then pile into the wagon bed of the buckboard, which had a bed of hay to cushion our lumpy, bumpy ride.

As the fall season was settling in, the daylight hours were getting shorter. Mother was busy putting up some canned soup with the last of our garden vegetables, along with some plum butter, using what plums were left on our fruit trees. With each passing day we were hoping to hear from Father soon.

CHAPTER 20

Father's Coming

One morning after the postman passed, a letter came with an announcement. Father was coming. Mother began cleaning the nest while we scurried about anticipating all that we would share with him. Mother threatened to tar and feather us if we didn't calm down and quit our shenanigans. Without a calendar or a radio, we lost track of time. The news of his arrival placed us in a magical fog. Anxiety and desire to see our father again was met with uncontrollable anticipation. We hoped that it would not rain and knock out the low bridge, which was always a disaster when it rained.

During the interim, Mother decided to call upon a near neighbor for a visit. Sometimes visiting a neighbor meant splendid things, and sometimes it meant un-splendid things. Nonetheless, we needed to take along the necessities such as water and a faithful lantern. Mother tucked in her basket a tasty bit of plum butter for a hospitality gift.

FATHER'S COMING

Junior tested the wick on the kerosene lantern. This was his assigned job. If a wayward cloud kept us from returning in the light of the moon, it would mean total blackout. Traveling back in total darkness might cause us to get lost. People seldom ventured out after dark. Armed with only a trusted lantern and some plum butter, we tromped to our dear neighbor's house.

To keep up the pace, we walked fast and furious. "Where are we going, Mother? Where are we going?" would be the usual questions of conversation.

"Never mind, never mind," was the usual quotable answer.

Uncle Joshua's place was in the direction of where we were headed, and I captured Mother's attention with this fact. I knew exactly which direction we had come from, as we plodded onward. We hoped that this time Uncle Josh would be somewhere around. I crossed my fingers. I was hopeful to meet him and wondered if he was back from sailing on the seven seas.

Approaching the sassafras fields, one felt the grass roots of the jungle foliage underfoot. "Uncle, Uncle," we cried in harmony, and lo and behold the magic door opened. Here before us was good old Uncle Josh, our host. We greeted our salty sailing family fellow, who was the famous radio doctor and keeper of the keys to the cabin. Mother beamed with pride as she introduced her little tribe to Uncle Josh, proper like. I could see Uncle was most happy in spite of my startled staring, with my mouth wide open. He was downright friendly but built like an elf. He was miserably freaked by a fall from a highchair and looked like a seahorse in shape. He seemed self-conscious and timidly shy. He resembled Mother in the face and appeared more Indian than I had imagined. He had on tiny little pants. He seemed to have a hump on his back and a hump on his chest, which made his head look like a turtle's tucked in between the two humps where they connected.

"I'm not in pain, child," he spoke kindly and with understanding. I guess my rudeness was plain to see. Mother always said it was rude to stare, and I was certainly staring.

"I'm sorry, Uncle, I didn't mean to be impolite," I apologized.

"After you get to know me well, you won't feel bothered. Most people around here overlook my misshapen form. After a while you will feel comfortable and completely at ease," Uncle Josh remarked. I felt bad that I had possibly hurt his feelings. I was small and ignorant, and I knew that I'd better make a decent retreat. A silent getaway outside his cabin beckoned, for inside was hardly big enough for visiting. I stepped beyond the big door and released my tensions.

"That's right, make yourself at home. I have a very big yard. There are lots of nice flowers to pick and choose from if you like wildflowers, children," he called out the door.

As I made a decent departure, Mother began to converse quietly. I searched for the others who were running wild and having a picnic in Uncle's backyard. The cabin door remained ajar, and I could see Uncle was busily tinkering and toying with the radio on his table. The radio seemed to be violently sick. It popped and cracked and backfired like Mr. Keyser's Model T.

After a short visit, we said our proper goodbyes to our newly found uncle. Our immediate departure left us with the hope that we would meet again soon. With Uncle waving his short arms in the air like a cheerleader, he shouted, "Come back real soon."

Mother called back to her little crippled brother, "That I'll do, that I'll do."

Proceeding onward, Mother had kept the worst of her business from us. We did not know until we arrived that we were going to visit a neighbor who had lost her daughter. As we entered the little shack-like residence, the sun was going down in the west.

The darkened house was lit by the flickering of a small candle, which cast a creepy-looking shadow throughout the small room. The candle had almost burned itself out. The furniture appeared rude and rough and really much too big for the room. In one corner was a strange-looking box-like coffin. It was braced across two chairs with low seats and high ladder backs. The room reeked with the smell of tallow from the burning candle. It was most unpleasant. I felt uncomfortable. I wanted to turn and run.

"It was good of you to come, Minnie, but such a long way. You really shouldn't have, you know," the old woman was speaking. As she was commenting, she wiped her eyes with the corner of her apron. "You have your hands full with your four little ones. How do you make out in these poor times?" Mother had hardly a chance to answer the question before the woman began to speak again. "My daughter was such a good girl, only sick with a fever a few days. Doctor said she'd pull through, and she'd be fine in a day or so. Then the other day, she started to refuse to eat and drink and suddenly passed on quietly in her sleep without a whimper."

Mother tried to give the woman strength of encouragement with words of condolences. "I'm so sorry; it's a real shame. Just can't explain why these things have to happen, but they can't be avoided I guess. I buried a little one myself, just a baby. It just didn't seem right, but we must not question the Lord. He knows what is best for us."

"I think that medicine done killed her, Minnie. That doctor would be better off taking care of horses and leaving innocent people alone. You know, Minnie, that doctor puts away a jug of Apple Jack almost every day. He stays corned up most of the time. He ought to have better sense," the old woman just rambled on and on. As I listened to the drifting conversation, I cringed a little inside; another doctor for my list.

The room was dark, and I could barely see now that the sun had set. The lit candle made the shadows look longer, as they spread out like huge ghosts behind the furniture. This lady was really poor. She didn't even have kerosene light like we had. Mother always said there is always someone poorer than the next, and she was right.

My nose began to crinkle from the smell of the fumes of the burning candle. As the women conversed in low tones, I decided to take a walk to the coffin and peek inside. The others followed me over to the chairs to view the body. Evidently, this lady's daughter was too long for her coffin box. She was crammed into her insufficient space with barely enough room for her legs. Laid out in her plain cotton dress, her corpse was half uncovered. Her hands were placed together in an overlapping manner.

I bravely reached into the coffin to feel the skin as Mother, who must've spotted my action, snapped at me, "Keep hands off, Eleanor, that's not necessary." Mother was giving me an order in a demanding voice. Quickly I pulled my arm back, but not before I finished what I had intended to do in the first place. My quick completion was observed, and I caught that certain look of Mother's forbidding eyes. I knew she was unhappy about my curiosity. It was something I could not control.

We didn't stay much longer, as Mother informed the lady that we had to be on our way. The darkness outside and the soft dusty roads would now be embracing us. I refused to prolong my captivity within these walls of this little place any further, so I stepped outside.

Looking back through the doorway of this simple, shabby house, I saw two women both firmly grasping each other's hand in a friendly, sad parting farewell. Mother had expressed her condolences with sincere sympathy for her daughter's passing. She left her gift of sweet plum butter to dissolve the bitterness on the tongue from the taste of sorrow in death, that only time could heal.

Parting the dust in the road with our bare feet, we toyed with time, as we waited impatiently for Mother to get on her high horse and head back to the hills. It was like a thoroughbred race at the horse park, with anxiously harnessed horses straining at the gates ready to set the pace and gallop off toward a finish.

Mother suddenly appeared, and she was off and running. We would find ourselves frantically running amok and behind.

As we journeyed down the road, I began playing devil's advocate leaping into lengthy questions, asking Mother, "Why was that girl's skin so different from June's skin?" Her skin was soft, but June's skin was hard and cold.

Mother replied, "Eleanor, you ask the darndest questions. Can't you leave well enough alone?" Mother seemed noticeably perturbed. As we proceeded homeward, I was looking for a little loophole in opportunity to try and inquire again.

"Are we headed for home? Where are the Keysers' cattle? Did they roam?" I blurted out.

We trotted along, as the dirt squished between my bare feet like fine brown sand sifting through my toes. It was plain to see that the water-filled ditches, which usually plagued the roads, were dehydrated. However, the beaten path still brought fear from the culverts. This was real rugged country with many menacing dangers. There was poison ivy draped in full view where any little explorer could be deceived by the finery. There were leaves of sumac disguised with white berries that even dandelions dared not to dance alongside of. Mother took every opportunity to fill in the blank spaces of silence with a conversational caution or two. She was well aware of these despicable dangers on display.

Knowing that I wouldn't give up easily, Mother let me ramble on. "Can you tell me why, Mother? I want to know," I demanded in a soft-sell manner. My provocative reasoning was not to be taken lightly as she decided to give in.

"Didn't your father explain about embalming fluid?" I knew that embalming fluid had created a funny odor around June's body. Father had explained it was due to the smell of death, which was customary in most funeral parlors. I pondered how this would apply to this circumstance.

"Yes," I replied with some satisfaction.

"Well," she continued, "this child's mother did not have any money for embalming fluid. Her coffin was homemade from the wood her father cut and built himself. She is just as she was in life only her heart stopped beating. She is not preserved."

Then Mother, who was probably primed by my pumping questions, went on explaining, "Your father had no money for embalming or a coffin, but things are done differently in the big city. When June was buried, she was placed in an unmarked grave in the Potters Field section because we too had no money. Lord only knows, we still owe that funeral man and may never get him properly paid." I was not always able to understand Mother, although I tried. Her words would seem to hang on and on, and somewhere my hearing apparatus, always being wired and plugged into my emotions, would somehow move on.

Soon after that eventful afternoon, Father arrived on the designated day, meeting us at the picket fence. We were dancing around in delight with circus performer skill, all participating in acrobatics. We proceeded to hang from the old mulberry tree and provided a burlesque show of busybodies parading before his attention. An amateur demonstration of how to milk a cow, with one hand behind the back, was first on the agenda, followed by lessons on how to ride old Rose's calf. We entertained him with the death-defying act of catching a reckless red-nosed rooster, and thrilled him with the taming of our wild beast incarnate in the poor old dog, Tootsie, who remained underneath the arches of the porch out of the sun. All this was then followed by a rousing chorus of barnyard sounds.

Father was more than impressed by our feats of courage and our cheerful child chatter. Mother smugly remained silent like a cat that just swallowed the canary, while we captured Father's attention with our impromptu antics.

After we simmered down, Father began to fall into the spirit of things. He grabbed his case, as we anxiously awaited the surprising trinkets and treasures in his bulging bag of promise.

The fine old cowhide satchel was handsomely chiseled with the wear and tear crushed-leather look. Few could afford this kind of sporty accessory. It gave off a delicious, friendly odor. The latch snapped open and came to attention, as the aroma encircled our heads like a wreath.

Father's trusty case stirred up my imagination. I envisioned him being a secret spy returning from a mission after receiving his payola. We gathered around, positioning ourselves on the floor. Father stood front and center. We were four little Indians and one Indian squaw. He became our Great White Chief, and he began to speak, "This case belonged to my father, and I have carried it a long way from the hills of Pennsylvania to the mountains of Detroit, and now here to the molehill of Mount Erie. If this case could only talk, it would tell many tales about the ties, socks and underwear it enjoyed carrying." Father spoke softly, as he sorted through articles he was unpacking. Reaching down into the bottom, Father turned to look at Mother as he slowly pulled his arm back from the depths of the bottomless pile of packages within. As a storyteller, he enjoyed keeping us in the state of suspense.

When Father's arm emerged from the dutiful leather case, he was holding a white box tied with a big red ribbon. The name Fannie May was boldly printed across the top. It was a box of chocolates and Mother's favorite kind. Mother reached for the box of chocolates and blushed like a new bride. It was obvious she was not the forgotten woman she sometimes thought she was. Little Juanita received her present first. Father handed her a little rubber ball and a paperweight filled with water with a snow scene. When shaken, the little treasure produced a lively snowy scene artificially flaky but most certainly realistic. Father cautioned her about breakage and dropping the snow bowl on her toe.

Junior cried, "What's for me?" as he screamed with glee. He was told to wait and see. Father reached in again and pulled out a small flat box tied securely. Inside the package were soldiers made of lead and a beautiful Red Scout pocketknife. Junior threw his arms around Father and joyfully exclaimed, "It's just what I wanted, Father."

Father reached in the case again. This time it was for Velma's present. She tore open the package and crayons fell out alongside a large thick coloring book and some hair bows. Somehow I was enjoying the others, as I watched them receive their gifts. Soon, the floor began to fill with wrapping paper scraps and string.

Father reached once more into his case, he had saved my gift for last, "Because," he said, "you are the oldest." He pulled out a parcel of peppermint sticks that resembled a barber pole with gray and red and white stripes. I twirled them between my fingers. Then Father pulled out a freshly laundered shirt. "That's not for me, Father, is it? You're just stalling to keep me guessing, aren't you?" I was a bit worried, but Father, who could be a bit of a tease sometimes, reached back into his case searching under the sock and underwear compartment and pulled out a rather heavy package. He handed it to me. I eagerly tore open the package, and there inside was a wonderful book of children's stories. Father knew how much I loved books. In addition to my book, I also received a nice, shiny new pen.

Then Father reached down one more time and said, "I almost forgot. I have one more thing." He handed me a giant jar of library paste. He knew that pasting in my scrapbook was my most favorite pastime. I was always pasting something. Father warned me, "Don't eat that stuff or put it in your mouth," as he turned quickly to Velma who had opened it and applied some of the good smelling paste on her finger and proceeded to lick a sample. Again Father repeated his words of caution. "It may smell like chewing gum, but it's poisonous to the stomach," in his attempt to detour Velma from having her fun.

These presents must have set Father back at least a couple pairs of half soles for his own shoes. Father had on many occasions reminded us that he hadn't forgotten the ponies he had promised and the playhouses he had drawn on our tablets, but his shortcomings spoke of other things.

Father then took a long look noticing our hair. Mother had given us haircuts, Indian style. We were shapelessly shorn and looked a wee bit laddish. It was no doubt a good thing that we had no mirrors around. Father just shook his head and the matter was completely dropped.

Later that afternoon, the nearby neighbors dropped in for a brisk spot of tea; seems Father's arrival stirred up some fussing. They all had to come see Mr. Snyder, Minnie's man, for it was Father's first trip to Mother's territory. The neighbors were always friendly, and when they came a calling, they would set quite a spell, sometimes wearing down the welcome mat.

The neighbors to the west of us were Mr. and Mrs. Hill. As far as anyone could tell, they had no living children and were extremely aged. Mr. Hill was a man whose back was severely and uncommonly bent over from pushing a walking plow. He could not rightly hold his head up to speak properly. Mrs. Hill was also bent in back, but she was as round as a washtub and plump in the cheeks. She seemed jolly enough, but she was nursing a disturbing habit. She was addicted to chewing coffee grounds.

When Mrs. Hill came to visit, she insisted on baking "a right nice cake for Mr. Snyder," whom she thought was an extremely "pretty man," as she put it. Sitting next to Mrs. Hill, caused me great distress, for the smell of her coffee breath made me ill. Coffee breath was a pet peeve of mine, ever since meeting Lady Delilah at the apartment building. I could not stand that pungent odor. Mrs. Hill's cud-like chewing disturbed my thoughts and brought back memories. I could no longer bear to sit next to her and made a fast retreat.

"Minnie, I'll have that cake ready in no time at all, and I want you to send one of the girls up to fetch it," she went on. Mother replied, "That's too much for you and it's not necessary, but if you insist." Mother did not make cakes. I don't know why. Maybe she didn't know how, but she sure knew how to cobble a pie.

I knew full well that I would be the one to go obtain this masterpiece. Mrs. Hill needed time to get it properly in and out of the oven. Mrs. Hill could surely bake. I know because many times she offered up a sample taste. She was a dear lady who loved children. Her only fault, sad but true, was her need to chew coffee grounds. It was a real smile breaker.

FATHER'S COMING

The following day arrived, and I was elected to the charge of the cake take. Now we all know what can happen when an office is filled by an untrustworthy public servant, one who takes part of the till, who tests the frosting so to speak, and leaves the tracings of his guilty fingerprints in a tiny suspicious trail throughout his thundering, blundering term.

Thus, it was the tale of the tempting topped treat which I was supposed to bring back safely to my mother's kitchen. Being duly swept into office by an overwhelming vote, I created what might be termed a landslide, which in turn could be viewed as a lop-side. By the time I reached the end of my term in office and returned to the official gods of my people, I found I was tempted, tested and tried. I found the treat sweet to eat. I kept taking a little bit more, just a little bit more, just a little bit more. Before I realized what had happened, the top and the sides were lopsided and my fingerprints were deeply embedded in the topping.

Well, my overdrawn account was in a sticky situation and was soon discovered by my auditor. I was immediately called up before the board for a meeting, with the critical evidence on my face. In my own defense, I had no rhyme or reason. I had tried to lick the damaging evidence from my fingers, but I had failed to remove incriminating fingerprints. The verdict was guilty, although I pleaded innocent. The Commissioner tried to defend my honor, but I was quickly removed from my office, depriving me of any future opportunities to try this again anytime soon.

I threw myself on the mercy of the court, and with much deliberation they granted a reprieve, while the meek, curious eyes of the jury looked on. No further judgments were made, and the treat was resurrected for reasonable raffle.

Well, I obviously established a record. A sorry mess to be sure, but I was forgiven for this political smear, and washing my hands helped clear it all up. I had been granted grace from my parents. Mother proceeded to put the kettle on, and we all had soup followed by the remainder of this delightful cake.

The rest of the evening went well despite my record in the chocolate court. Father realized our active day had Mother mumbling for the miracle of bedtime. Strangely, Father began looking for a prop for the door.

Mother eyed him and said, "What are you doing that for?"

"Locking the door," was his simple reply. "It's a practice I initiate as a caution."

"Heaven's sake, you don't have to lock doors out here. You're just being silly. Leave the door alone, and let's go to bed," Mother directed.

Father was determined to brace the door with a prop and wouldn't put it down.

"Now look here, Cecil, don't start that foolishness. You'll frighten the kids," Mother proclaimed.

"Well," Father replied, "it's just that a little precaution is worth a pound of cure." Father's intentions were pure.

Mother slowly walked over and removed the trap from the doorknob. "What have we got to lose? We have nothing." It was true. We were really poor. Father's reason for wanting to lock the door was a force of habit. Quite frankly, locking the door was completely out of the ordinary for country living. A measure such as this was quite proper for city life. Father didn't believe in taking chances. His bold advances earned him a big fat zero.

We sat on the floor watching Mother unbolt the door that Father had just fixed. Mother stated, "We don't have prowlers out here, just cats in the night and the mouse squad who usually end up sleeping in the potato bin. No one is out after dark. For goodness sakes, the common chickens in the hills are better watchdogs and quite capable of making terrible fusses if a stranger were to sneak in."

Father's administration was short lived, for Mother, who became Mrs. Right, electing herself as the expert of the hour, settled the matter. She had gotten her way. The less said the better beamed from Father's shy grin. He knew when to leave well enough alone and we mounted the stairs, heading off to bed.

The next day Mr. Keyser came by for a visit. The two men had never met, and a real fine welcome carpet was unfolded. Father, who was of the city flavor, borrowed a pair of Sam Keyser's oldest son's cowpoke pants. Before the cock had crowed the next morning, Father was up and dressed, headed down the road toward Sam Keyser's place. He wanted to pitch in with the chores. He took to flinging hay, but Sam saw Father had limitations with his herniated groin, and called upon his sons to finish transferring the hay from the back of the buckboard to the barn.

With those limitations in mind, attention was then given to the tryout of milking the cow. Father, who was in thinking mode, noticed that the condition of milking was done ordinarily in unsanitary, unsatisfactory, and uncontrolled environments. With this in mind, the seed was planted in preparation for a new invention. The Keysers' cows were clearly the mechanism of yet another honest-to-goodness invention idea.

Mr. Keyser was not fully aware that his barn was unsanitary, as Father poked at his cow's conditions. Mr. Keyser was willing to try to accept any proposal that could change his operation for the better. Father promised him that he would work the project out on paper as soon as he returned to the city. In the back of Father's mind, he was dwelling on something official to improve milking conditions. He told Sam that it might take a while to devise a plan and advised Sam that he had nothing yet, but he would come up with a surprise in the very near future. It was just like Father to see something wrong that needed fixing and then want to fix it.

Already Father and Sam Keyser were two men brought together in a common bond. Father's popularity pool, long may it wave, was enticing another fan. During the next few days, Father's lily-white hands and paleface skin started to take on a healthy glow. Time was passing much too quickly. Father knew that he must return to the lobbying forces back in Chicago.

Father's last night, before parting, remains indelibly in my memory. Many times, Mother had accused Father of being afraid of his own shadow. On this memorable night, as the moonlight disappeared and the darkness knelt beside our little frame house, we began our parade up the stairs. Father demanded to be the leader to prove to us children that he was not afraid of the dark. As we mounted the stairwell, Mother noted a word of caution in the direction of the front of the line and warned against any foolishness, citing a need to proceed with care. Mother brought up the rear. She then blew out the kerosene lamp and the lingering smell floated on the airwaves in the tiny room. The smell seemed to last forever.

As we settled down in our straw bed pallets, the quiet was shattered by a soft knocking sound. Father was alarmed and made a big fuss as he sat up in bed. He pitifully cried, "Minnie, Minnie, there's someone downstairs. Go down and find out who it is." His command fell on silent ears. Mother was either asleep or pretending not to hear.

About this time, a strong dull thudding hit the unconventional porch below. "Minnie, are you asleep?" Father seemed worried. "Did you hear that?" Father was pushing for an answer.

"Hear what?" Mother retorted in an unconcerned manner.

"That noise downstairs, someone's trying to get in the door." This time Father was certainly convinced.

Mother took her sweet time about coming up with any answers for his persistent questions. "Why don't you go down and see who it is, Minnie?" Father was now getting a bit loud.

"If you're so interested, why don't you go?" Mother remarked. "I'm not worried the least bit," she added.

"Well," Father assured her, "it's just that I'm a stranger here and they would know you much better than me." Father seemed really upset. I could tell that Mother was getting perturbed.

"Oh, go to sleep, for heaven sakes. It's probably nothing."

Father was not convinced, "Something is making that muffled banging sound."

"Oh, alright, I'll go check, but it is just plain crazy." Mother crept out of bed and without lighting the lamp, she tiptoed down the stairs to see what she could see. She knew full well that Father was making a to-do about nothing. I could hear her mumbling, as she stepped softly in her bare feet on the bare boards of the stairway.

Upon her return, she announced to Father that all was well. "I was right," she stated. "That noise you heard was old Rose knocking around the porch steps with her clumsy hoofs."

Father blurted out, "Well it could've been a man with hip boots on or at least that's what it sounded like to me."

Mother responded, "Rose is just a friendly dairy cow. She is playful and can't stay where she belongs. She is worse at night when she prowls a path near the porch. The kids spoil her by giving her corn by the front door, and she doesn't know any better at night."

Father chimed in, "Well you ought to put a bell on her, and then you would know where she is and what she's doing at night." Father was feeling rather silly and realized he had brought down disgrace on his own head, having crawled under the covers.

Rose was harmless and gentle, but a noisy busybody. One night before Father had arrived, she had overturned the washbasin on the front porch with her hooves, which caused us to be suddenly startled, but after that she couldn't fool us anymore. Mother gave Father a whole spiel about poor old Rose's noisy nonsense at night, and Father's fears were put to rest, as I wearily drifted off.

The liberties Father had taken with our bedtime were apparent the following morning when we all overslept. The daylight was glaring and was making our cock-a-doodle-doer crow. The barnyard was coming to life, awakening the family. Ducks were quacking for feed, while the cat had gotten into the chicken house and was rustling up the hens that were resting on our breakfast eggs. The chickens were squawking, and old Rose was giving her moos, while her calf was busy scratching her backside against the latched gate, making a rattling noise.

It was a crisp, cool, carefree morning, as the act of coming to life was in progress. We rubbed the sleep from our eyes, knowing full well this was Father's last day. We selfishly felt we had already lost too much time by our overindulgence in pillow pounding. It was as though he was leaving the earth and we would never see him again. As Father walked forward, we followed him by stepping in his footprints, and together we headed for breakfast.

We did not want Father to leave, even though he explained he could no longer stay with us. Junior was reaching out for companionship from Father, but Father could not cater, for he needed to return to Chicago to continue the fight for justice.

Mother's resourcefulness and accomplishments over the past months received Father's highest praise, even though she was a might off on her haircutting skills. Father agreed the country was good for children, and he was glad that Mother had found this place.

With our dog wagging his tail, we gathered up Father's things and proceeded to make ready for his official departure back to Chicago. With tears overflowing the banks of our eyes, we gave backhanded swipes to the tears streaming down our cheeks. We were not very good at saying goodbye, not even in Indian style. Father promised to get things rolling so that we could all be together again. But for now, we had to hang on for a little while longer. "Give my regards to the Keysers, and I'll be writing soon to let you in on current events," Father announced, and then he left for the city. Our mood was mighty dispirited. Mother did her best to lift our spirits.

CHAPTER 21

Lessons Run Amok

Right after Father's departure, Halloween crept into our cranny. Mother was preparing for a little celebration. It was a chilly evening that Halloween. I shiver to think of it now. Mother invited a few neighbors over for a box supper. A box supper meant you brought your own fried chicken or cake or pie and shared it with everyone. It was a very common way to have a party, especially when one is too poor to furnish refreshments.

We built a small campfire in the same spot where Father's had been several days prior. After the neighbors left, Junior took charge of the leftover smoldering embers. We gathered around in a squatting position and held our hands over the flameless fire. We were speaking about Father's trip back to Chicago and wondering when we would receive our invitation back to the city.

Our bedtime passed without notice, and Mother's attention was taken up with conniving us to get into the house. Our late bedtime hour was striking a blow past the eleventh hour, and her

LESSONS RUN AMOK

attempts went unheeded. Without announcing her intentions, which was the usual procedure, she secretly slipped inside and covered herself with a sheet from the bed. She then proceeded around to the back of the house. In a sneaky, stalking stride, she slowly appeared from the blackness, sneaking up from behind. I spotted a white, wiggly wisp advancing. Then suddenly, it stopped short and stood stretched out like a spirit in soulless flight. It was only a matter of seconds before adrenaline kicked in. In pure panic and bedlam, we ran screaming, nearly killing each other trying to get to the house, charging the front door.

"Mother, Mother! Where are you? There's a ghost, a real ghost, out there in the yard," we all yelled at the top of our lungs. We flew through the house in a frantic search for Mother, but we were unable to find her. We soon recognized what was taking place. Mother was mysteriously missing.

Seconds later, Mother appeared at the door carrying a sheet over her arm. "What's all the fuss about? Did someone call me?" Mother seemed much too calm.

We eyed her carefully before accusing her. "It was you, Mother. You were the one in that sheet. I saw your feet."

Actually, no one really knew who was in that sheet. We all scattered for the hills so fast that there was no time to look at anything. I was the least brave, but I was smart enough to see that Mother had some pretty incriminating evidence on her arm.

It was the joke of the month, and Mother would not soon let us forget. It took a good long time before we got over this bewitching. Mother smiled her famous smile, emphasizing a revealing lesson, and through our agony quoted, "It was all worthwhile."

That same month we started school. We were entered into a one-room schoolhouse. Mr. Keysers' relative, Mr. Eldo Fitch, was the stern schoolmaster. He taught readin', writin' and 'rithmatic.

He rode his spirited horse to school each morning, laying upon his trusty steed only a few lashes. He was a hot-rodder all cloaked in his cape, riding on the back of his horse. He wore a funny Amish-type hat on his head. His character resembled a tall jockey, as he bent forward in his squeaky saddle to meet the whirl of the wind head on. His spooky ride each morning was more than one could imagine. He always left a dusty cloud trailing behind, concealing the path on the way to school.

One day, we mischievously mobilized in a ditch for an all-out attack on his person. Hiding deep down inside a culvert along the road, the older boys yelled, "Eldo Fitch is a mean old snitch." Naturally we followed suit and chimed in. Somehow, Mother found out about our little prank, and we were firmly reprimanded in no uncertain terms.

Remembering this lesson, the next school day, we meandered toward the schoolhouse carrying our familiar lard buckets filled with plum jam sandwiches. Our schoolhouse was small and consisted of a few desks, a pointing stick, a rollup map and two blackboards. Each child owned his own books, his own lard bucket and a sharp pencil. Books were guarded and passed from one to another, in a hand-me-down fashion. The Keysers, who had practically one book for every grade in the system, loaned them to us.

Teachers were never screened for their methods of discipline. A long, wooden yardstick ruler would serve as a measuring tool and an instrument of choice for infractions. It was the Master's minding maker. All teachers were rigid, and school rules were usually quite acceptable to parents. I say usually, for there are always exceptions to every rule, and invariably I would turn out to be that exception.

LESSONS RUN AMOK

If a child needed a sample of proper discipline, he was sure to find the policy of physical punishment tough. A teacher could carry out specific plans and measures at his disposal, all without permission from parents at home. If you got it good at school you dare not go home and tell your parents or you'd more than likely get another dose of what ails you at home. At least that was the usual procedure. Needless to say, I had not been informed of any procedures, but I was about to find out.

Schoolmaster Fitch believed in swatting. He never wasted time tapping and rapping a child with a ruler. No, he would swat your backside after a fruitless attempt at reciting. He'd display his trusty horse whip as a weapon, hanging it on the wall in plain view as a warning. Few children dared to invite this type of punishment, especially if they had experienced it previously. Somehow, I failed to get the message.

One day as recess time was approaching, a naughty classmate threw my composition book out the little frame window into the schoolyard. Without thinking, I ran to the window and leaned over toward the ground and tried with all my might to retrieve the thing. Mr. Fitch had not seen the composition book fly out the window, but he definitely spotted my rump in the air from inside the room. Without warning he wailed the whip against my upturned bottom. I went sailing right out the window. I refused to be intimidated by his way, and I was automatically labeled defiant.

That afternoon after school, he made me stay after class and paddled me with the yardstick ruler in a mechanical centrifugal movement. Round and round we went. I danced a jig to the tune of Eldo Fitch. Crying and pulling away from the stern master only made him more resolved. I cried all the way home. When I burst upon Mother, I frantically told her all that Mr. Fitch had done. She did seem concerned, but I could not tell whether or not she was on my side. The next day, she told me she would have a talk with Mr. Keyser. I did not ever return to that school again. From then on out, I did my silent study at home.

Shortly after I had been removed from school, Mother hitchhiked back to Chicago leaving us in the care of the Keysers. We moved from our little home we shared with Mother into the Keysers' home. While Mother was away, we did our daily chores and endeavors. We broke bread, did our ritual bathing of tired feet, and we chattered by the lamplight in preparation for bedtime.

Another day was finished when we mounted the attic staircase with our hot bricks to place under our patchwork quilts on our soft feather beds. It was a far cry from the pallets of straw placed on the floor in the home we shared with Mother. Having moved in with the Keysers, we would now be presided over by their loving care, while both our parents were gone.

We were slowly growing more accustomed to our new home each day. Then one day, the Keysers' mean old dog, Rover, lay in wait. He was usually shut up in the corn crib when his services were not needed, out of fear that he would put his teeth marks in one's legs. I had a terrible feeling that one day he would nip me, and I was right. His jaws were the size of a bear trap, and his teeth were sharp enough to make a cow dance when he barked his authority alongside of them. He was a valuable dog to any farmer, and his mean jealousy was permissible because he was a work dog.

He sized me up, one unsuspecting day, as I left the barn area. I had been playing in the hay loft. As I climbed down, he cornered me and attacked me from the rear. Rover snuck up and bit me on the behind. It was so fast and furious that I felt no pain at the moment of impact. However, this attack caused me to lose control of my bladder and created much embarrassment. This was way more painful.

LESSONS RUN AMOK

Mrs. Keyser felt deeply sorry about the accident and took her shoe off and threw it at old Rover. She ran after him and cornered him in the corn crib where he was then locked up for his belligerence. I can still see, in my mind's eye, the picture of Mrs. Keyser running after this miserable beast. Rover took off with Mrs. Keyser running after him. She chased him all the way back to the corn crib and limped back on one shoe. I couldn't help but laugh. It took almost an hour to find the blasted shoe which she had thrown at Rover.

My wounds healed and life went on. Then one day our parents sent notice requesting our return. Our salty tears mingled for a moment, as we said our goodbyes. We were then sent back to our familiar impoverished lifestyle back in the city.

CHAPTER 22

The Return

Father was still plugging along in the only existence he knew at the apartment building working on the Lindbergh case and the reorganization of his business. The newspapers were having a field day with the Lindbergh kidnapping stories, which seemed to go on and on, year after year.

Some newspapers published slanderous stories about Father; *The Chicago Herald and Examiner*, Thursday January 16, 1936, and *The Daily Times Chicago*, Thursday January 16, 1936, published an article titled: "Bruno Offered Hope By Two Chicago Clues:" mentions Father as a petty racketeer convicted in Detroit in 1928 under the Michigan Blue Sky Law. It mentions Snyder actually being involved in the kidnapping plot. And *The Chicago Herald and Examiner* talked about Cecil Snyder's torn pants on the kidnap ladder.

The Chicago Herald and Examiner, on Friday January 17, 1936, referred to him as a gangster and a petty racketeer. Under the heading "Cusack Explains," it reads as follows: "Lieut. William Cusack brought Cecil Snyder to his home in the month of April 1932. Lieut. Cusack does not deny this. He grins and explains, 'These two birds—Snyder and Davis—were both a little off center on the Lindbergh kidnapping—hipped, if you know what I mean. So, to get rid of Snyder, I brought him to Davis. That way, I got rid of two birds with one stone'." The authorities seemed to want to discredit Snyder and connect him with Davis, a suspected liar.

In the face of all that was against him, Father would not give up the ghost and quit. He did briefly threaten to sue a couple of the newspapers, but his penniless position of protest was in vain. He began saving articles in which libelous things were printed. Before long, the closets were overwhelmed with clippings contained in bushel baskets of collected sections from the newspapers.

I began making a scrapbook of my father's notable and notorious publicity. The freedom of the press is remarkable if not worthy of notice for their exploitation of a person's character. The inferences and accusations they exploit is absolutely despicable, if not sinful. Father did become duly obsessed with his clipping sessions and rightly so, for it just about ruined the whole family. Mother thought Father was losing his mind.

Years before, these same newspapers published articles complimenting him on his unique invention. He could not understand why they now took the stand against him, blasting his character and his honest, forthright intentions. His life work was conceived solely by him for the exact purpose of eliminating crime in the automobile industry. Murder, crime, and even corruption in politics were all things Father stood up against. He had a deep concern for law and order and was a dedicated person.

But, the newspapers now told an entirely different story. Cecil L. Snyder was being portrayed as a scoundrel in the sediments of glaring newspaper articles. Father refused to be intimidated by their accusations or allegations.

Unfortunately, there were other negative effects from Father's name being smeared all over the front pages. Being deprived of funds, Father was trying to put his business back on its feet. He was tremendously stressed and wearing thin, for he was suing the government and twenty-eight states for the exact sum of two billion dollars. Now that may sound funny, but Father had the biggest patent monopoly in the world, and he felt it was a fair sum. With our names on the lips of every outside influence in the neighborhood, our immediate family found ourselves becoming targets.

When Mother went to enroll us at the principal's office, she had to fill out forms. In completing those forms, information was required, like what is the father's occupation? Filling in the blank with inventor carried certain connotations. In addition, Mother was embarrassed when they raised their eyebrows and stared glassy-eyed, as she wrote that we were half Indian. Invariably, the questions would be asked, "What tribe are you from, and what did your husband invent?" Mother's situation was becoming one of shame. She did her best to try and shield us from the torment of children's attacks. Children would follow us home at night and torment us using phrases like, "If your old man is an inventor how come he's playing detective with kidnappers?" Or, "The only thing Snyder ever invented was catsup." It was discouraging at best. The children's crude remarks were minor, and Junior's black eyes were not too severe.

There were no shock absorbers available from the smear campaign of the newspapers. The sting of scandal was unbearable, and the bold headlines were devastating. This dilemma of overexposures and strange men who were constantly in our apartment transacting business, were overwhelming for Mother.

In order to get away from this smoke-filled environment and from discussions regarding the Lindbergh case, Mother called upon her organizational talents and moved us outdoors.

In our ventures outside, one would take notice of the streets which were crowded with mobs of people, who collected in small groups and listened intently to the original soapbox derby style speeches. If one wanted to know what the truth was, one only had to take to the streets. It was the outlet that was used to reveal President Roosevelt's schemes. The poor people hated Roosevelt for the way things were and blamed him for their plight.

These times didn't bother me, for I could overlook the immense squalor among the streets and the parks. However, I could not ignore the pigeon lady, who was in the park every single day feeding the white and gray pigeons. She seemed to know her feathered bird friends like the back of her hand. She carried a bag full of bread close to her miserably shabby caped dress that she wore. She not only appeared scandalously poor, but you could see she was a victim of old age and possibly had arthritis.

As a youth, age twelve, I found my immature moral sense excited with condemnation for her, while at the same time stirring my compassion in a pitiful merciful manner. Her crazy carpetbag was always sufficiently filled with scraps of bread for the birds. I pondered many times about the birds who had a crust of bread when we had none; a pigeon that had a tasty morsel for its supper while the poor were searching through waste containers for food, all while cursing Roosevelt.

Roosevelt was our shepherd all right, and we were wanting. People camped in front of shutdown factories and many strolled through back alleys for a place to sleep under some pile of newspapers. Yes, the poor were crying for relief. Poverty was short-circuiting everyone.

People were barely getting on with daily endeavors, hoping to obtain assistance from somewhere. Mother thought that the Welfare Department could help. She pleaded with Father to let the Welfare Department get him back up on his feet, but Father flatly refused. He did not want federal financing in any form. He would not permit Mother to go to work either, stating, "You are needed at home to care for the children."

The hand-to-mouth version of supplying groceries for the table was insurmountable.

Mother's milestones were evolving into possible gallstones, and Father's headaches were turning into Mother's heartaches. Everything came to a complete standstill. The final straw was manifested when an ultimatum was given by my mother. Things needed to change. After a mild confrontation, Mother staged a dramatic walkout. It remains painfully clear in my mind. Mother rose early as she was accustomed to doing and hurried us down the stairway. This day would become a memory full of strange emotions and the ultimate abandonment of our dear father, who stood dazed in disbelief at the top of the stairwell in his long underwear.

As I looked back at him standing there, he reminded me of a tall tree bent from the storms and buckling from the repeated bolts of lightning which struck him. The power of words, whether spoken or written, is incomprehensible. No one could have possibly foreseen that this would be the final collapse of our parents' relationship. From this day forward it would be the Welfare Department and Mother, an entirely new way of life. We had been uprooted many times before, but this time it would be the end of our family as we knew it.

CHAPTER 23

Separation

With the pleasant memories of the prior summer with the Keysers fading away, we were suffering from empty pockets. And with my father's scandalous newspaper articles becoming blotches on his bosom, Father was now a member of an untouchable class.

We were uprooted, being taken out of school, and transplanted, like a bunch of weeds, into a shelter. I would soon find out that life was going to be miserable. Shelters were common places for displaced women and children. No men were allowed. People who were housed in these shelters were there because they had no homes or were victims of eviction, while others were waiting for a job placement picked out for them by the government.

Mother had been promised by a welfare worker that she would be delivered from her present situation if she worked with the Welfare Department. In the end, she believed they would deliver the world on a silver platter. "A job is all you need to get you on your feet, Mrs. Snyder," they said. In her naivety, she believed every word they told her. She would constantly remind us that we were very lucky to be able to get help from the government, for the list was long.

It had only been a week, and Mother was busy applying for a domestic position in a big hotel in the Loop. The domestic position that she got was in actuality a scrub woman position.

Mother had to report every penny she made to the shelter. They in turn would deduct small amounts as payment for our extras. My sister, Juanita, was placed in a nursery. Velma and Junior were placed in a recess play group, and I was given library privileges. I spent most of my time doing the thing I loved most, reading one book after another.

Everyone slept in a dormitory-like room, on cots. Each and every morning we would be awakened by a matron ringing a bell through the hallway. After dressing, we would go over to the big house across the street and have breakfast, cafeteria style. Lunch was simple and we were served without Mother being present. In the evening we would be reunited with Mother when she returned from her employment. There was absolutely no place to go. Evenings had curfews. Everyone just sat around on cots and discussed the terrible times and shared a small bag of grapes or an apple, which was smuggled in. Most everyone hid their fruit in concealed corners and shoeboxes under the bed. Sometimes, we had to eat our extras after dark when the lights went out at nine o'clock.

Mother soon became well-established at her job. She sometimes would get permission to take me with her, to her job in the Loop, to help relieve my boredom. After nine months or more in the shelter, Mother was making enough money that the Welfare would now allow her to establish herself in her own place. Of course, this meant Mother would be under their watchful care and guidance. She was warned not to allow Father in her home at any time, or they would have to withdraw support, including any needed extras, like shoes and coats. The Legal Aid Department assured Mother that if Father dared to interfere or bother us children, she should notify them at once. They would take care of him legally.

Moving into our new place, things were still bleak, to say the least. Mother worked hard every day at the hotel. We were left to our own resources much of the time. Mother entrusted the care and safety of the younger ones to me. I was the oldest and was now in charge of overseeing them. While Mother was at work, Father would slip around to the nearest corner and secretly meet us. We would visit and talk under the eaves of some building canopy.

Father of course was very critical and did not like what was taking place. He said, "Your Mother is making a federal case of our personal business, and I've already got enough trouble with them as it is." Those were his sincere sentiments, and he made them known to us children. Of course, we carried this back to Mother. Most children would've done the same thing. We loved them both and could not see fault with either parent. We did not understand why things were the way they were.

Because Father did not like the situation surrounding us children, he began to make phone calls to Mother's supervisor. He would request that Minnie Snyder be sent home immediately, as she was badly needed at home. Mother would rush home, on several of these occasions, only to find what Father had done. She not only lost a day of pay, but eventually lost her job, being told by her supervisor to get her affairs in order at home. She was completely bitter about the disruption he was causing and needed to seek employment elsewhere. Mother felt she had no alternative. She went to the one place that promised to take measures against Father, the Welfare Department, because she felt harassed.

My Mother, who used to hum like a hummingbird around the house, was now gazing out the window, as if she were in a daze. She would talk to herself, having complete conversations. At first I observed this in a rather casual manner and would continue reading my book. After a while I would notice her venting. "That man! What he has done to me and these dear little children is more than one woman can bear," she would go on and on. Some days she would only do this for a matter of minutes. Then other days, she would be very upset. It became a matter of routine.

On one particular day, while Mother was scrubbing the floor and engaged in a lively conversation, talking to herself, I hesitantly approached her from behind and lightly tapped her on the shoulder. I asked, "Mother, who in the world are you talking to?" She became angry and growled at me, "Mind your own business." Mother's nerves were like the strings of a violin, so tightly tuned that they could pop. As a preteen, I was completely ignorant of what was causing these violent changes in Mother. I was worried beyond measure. I thought that if Mother could find more steady work maybe these behaviors would stop.

SEPARATION

Eleanor

Mother would spend whole days at the employment office waiting for another job placement. She would take most anything. It was considered lucky if you found a job working for someone who paid your wages, as well as your transportation fare. Once, Mother found a generous lady who gave her a few fairly decent dresses that no longer fit. She brought them home and cut them down so that we girls could wear them. Some of the dresses that were given to Mother were huge. We would wrap them around us and belt them off with a piece cut off from the bottom. We had nothing else to wear. The only new thing we had was a pair of shoes supplied by the Welfare Department once a year.

Now, a pair of shoes from the Welfare was mighty conservative. You went to a designated store and you were given what they wanted you to have. There was no choice of styles or color. Our stockings were also furnished by the Welfare. They were thick ribbed, dark brown cotton, so ugly and miserably uncomfortable. They were only good for warmth. We could not afford seasonal changes. The same stockings were worn year-round. In the summer, when it was hot out, you just rolled them down around the ankles, making them appear like huge doughnuts lying around your ankles. I hated them so much that sometimes I would remove them after leaving the house and go barelegged.

The Welfare Department was part of our daily lives, with the periodic checks they made. The well-intended government inspectors would come to our home and check up on us. There was no freedom from their pantry raids. This grand group of officials, who examined our living conditions with diligence and a friendly bedside manner, frequently punctuated our dismal gloom with hope. We would receive rations of dried apples, uncolored margarine, and a numbered brown paper sack neatly sealed with masking tape, containing our dry powdered milk supply.

Pathetically and ironically funny, we were thankful to God that we had water not only to bathe in and drink, but to bring the apples back to life and to change the water into milk. Oh how we missed our old friendly cow and the sweet tender plums from the fruit tree.

Our wounded lives were being bandaged courtesy of the Welfare Government. Yet, there were no quick fixes, just deprivation. The "twenty-three skidoo" era was gone, replaced by "Oh you great big beautiful doll." Only we had no dolls, no toys, no food, only periodicals. Most of the time we had no clothes or parents, not to mention a proper home or environment. A family who starves together stays hungry together. It is as plain as that. Without Father, we were in the care of the State of Illinois, wearing the ensemble look of the day, forlorn and crumpled.

Times were trying and although Mother was constantly keeping a vigil light burning in the employment department as a scrub woman, the fatal flaws of our system provided no recompense.

My beautiful Indian mother felt that her problem was due directly to Father. It was obvious; Mother was trying to face up to her tribulations as graciously as was possible. She worked when she could get a job, and when there was no work, she would resort back to the bread lines at the relief stations. There day-old bread was dispersed to the poor for pennies. Our rations were on a day-to-day basis and also from charity.

If Mother worked during the week, she would sometimes save a dime for us to go to the show on a Saturday. We would spend the whole day for a single dime in the theater. We also would walk to the library for our weekly exchange of books, making a whole day of this excursion. Mother was usually working or standing in line somewhere, so we'd have the entire day to ourselves.

On one particular Saturday, Velma and I walked to the Loop, accompanied by a girl named Bonnie, from our building. Upon reaching the Loop, we headed for our favorite big department store to take our weekly ride on the escalator. During one of these excursions, Velma found a handkerchief full of large green bills, mostly tens and twenties. The money was neatly tied in a little knapsack and contained no identifying information. It was more money than any of us had ever seen. It was a real wad of dough.

Without hesitation, we sought out a secluded alley along the street and divided up the loot. For the next few hours, we were busy filling two shopping bags apiece to the brim with some of the most ridiculous things one could imagine, anything that could be bought for money.

Unsupervised, we took advantage of this once-in-a-lifetime happening. We bought up everything in sight. Some of the things I remember purchasing were five different colors of ink and a real honest-to-goodness, one-of-each-color fountain pen. We bought gobs of candy that normally we could not afford and mounds of stationery and tablets for school. What was most surprising was not so much the way we shopped and what we purchased, but how cleverly we managed to get those tens and twenties cashed without creating suspicion. As children dressed like beggars, we were exchanging and breaking bills into smaller denominations in order to make purchases here and there.

Loaded down with our overflowing mammoth brown bags, we passed by a store window which sold greeting cards. It was nearing Valentine's Day and the window was full of assorted seductive choices of love messages. We went inside the little establishment and managed to blow almost twenty dollars on some of the silliest, most ridiculously priced pieces of paper ever printed on this green earth.

One card in particular caught my eye. I was fascinated with a captivating cow complete with eyelashes that opened and shut by pulling the little string attached in the back. Without rhyme or reason, I purchased that one at the small cost of one dollar, which was more money than Mother had for food in weeks. My extravagance was showing a bit, but it was not visible in my mirror of perspective. These artificial lashes of soft brown furry material, which successfully winked at me, attracted my fancy. Could it be I was subconsciously thinking of our old friendly cow Rose back on the farm?

It was a laborious ride home on a streetcar having to lug all those bags, but somehow we managed. All the way home, we cleverly cautioned Bonnie that she must swear to secrecy and never reveal how much we had found. By the time we reached the end of the line, Bonnie was thoroughly committed to secrecy.

Mother's measly money she received for a day's work looked rather slim compared to the stash we found. She wisely called our attention to the fact that we could not borrow or use other people's money. We first needed to find out who the money belonged to. This took us down a few pegs, as our treasure find was salted away until proper verification was made.

Meanwhile, Mother continued looking for steady work, and Father was busy seeking a sleeping room somewhere nearby. He managed to find one directly across the alley from the rear of our building.

Father lived close enough that he could pop up most anywhere or at any time, be it in the alley, under a building canopy or on the grounds across the street. He was faithful as the sun with his calls and visits. "Eleanor, Elean-ooo-rrr." His call in the back alley still rings in my ears to this day, like the morning cry of a wet bird seeking help from the downpour. This famous infamous call could be heard bouncing off the walls of the alleyway buildings, traveling upward to the third floor.

Our on-again off-again Welfare existence was a natural way of life for us. It seemed everyone we knew was on charity. I was unable to understand the reasoning concerning Mother's separation from Father. The fact that Father was not allowed in the home was unreasonable, and Mother's answer to this fact was because Father would not work. This reasoning was insufficient to me. I was always told Father was working because he said so. Being sometimes withdrawn in my own little world, I did not fully understand what was constantly disrupting our lives. Mother worked and Father worked; and yet we could never afford rent, food or clothes.

It seemed this way of life brought about Mother's behavior of constantly talking to herself. Or, she would seek an outside ear for an outlet to her mental strain. Many times, she would engage in conversation with perfect strangers, at the relief station or while standing in the breadline. Her pathetic stories never fell on a deaf ear. Mother's tongue beat a drum signaling turmoil from within.

We were sprouting like sprigs and eager to try to help Mother in every way. I tried to get a babysitting job, but these jobs were few. I did however manage to get one babysitting job right in the building after Mother did some mouth-to-mouth advertising about how trustworthy and reliable I was.

My first job, one evening, was taking care of two young babies. The children were put to bed early and were fast asleep when I arrived. Unfortunately, that evening was interrupted by a man's leg protruding through the first-floor window. I ran screaming

SEPARATION

in panic. By the time help arrived, the man got away. My future babysitting jobs were canceled thereafter. It would be a long time before Mother would permit me to try again.

My brother was also eager to help financially. Together we engaged in a full magazine route, hitting every Clark Street tavern with our sales abilities. We never came home until every last paper, from *The Liberty* to the *Saturday Evening Post*, was sold. I went to guard the little red wagon which held the surplus that could not be carried on our back. There was always some ruffian ready to steal a few. Even the newspaper boy at the corner could not turn his back for a second before someone with a long arm and sticky fingers tried to take a few papers.

When we weren't trying to assist Mother with finances, we were off visiting with Father, who sometimes entertained us in his room. Father's room was a wonderland full of gimmicks, strings, pulleys and lots of apparatuses.

Uniquely fascinating were the mobiles he had hanging around the room from little strings. I thought Father was ingenious with these masterpieces. I could not take my eyes off of them. His table was full of wonderful drawings and writings, and he always had a plentiful supply of Matzo crackers lying around. This was a real treat, for Mother refused to buy them.

After a visit with Father, we would return home and recount our adventures to Mother. She would listen in a disinterested fashion. Prolonged chatter on the subject would cause remarks such as, "Your father is nuts. He needs to get out and work to support you kids. All he does is fight with the government and the Welfare Department." Our reports back to Father about her disposition and disgruntled manner would bring a sad smile along with retorts of, "Your mother will never understand because she doesn't want to." And so it went, day in and day out.

Our visiting with Father provided the opportunity to make the acquaintances of two lovely Filipino landladies who Father rented from. They were the keepers of sleeping rooms for quiet respectable gentlemen. Miss Mickey was a bachelor lady. Her sister, Mary, was a student of music and practiced every day. We could hear her playing the piano when we would visit with Father. Frequently we would be invited in to sit in their parlor to listen to real classical piano interpretations. It was splendid. I could tell the ladies liked us children.

Miss Mickey and Miss Mary took a special interest in us girls. They invited us to attend a formal Filipino Ball which was held annually in a Loop hotel. Because Miss Mickey was a seamstress and Miss Mary did fancy tatting, they made us each a lovely dress to wear. It took much pleading to obtain permission from Mother in order to go, but we finally convinced her. We changed into beautiful dresses and were whisked away in a taxi, accompanied by two lovely ladies of culture. It was a wonderful fairytale dream come true. The barricades came down long enough for us to see a tiny glimpse of another world other than the one we were dwelling in. Velma and I felt like royalty.

CHAPTER 24

Cold Water Flats

Mother's plight was such that we needed to move again. This time it was down the street to the cold water flats. These places were pretty rough to live in. The only electricity in the building was a dimly lit 15-watt bulb, one on each floor, located near the coal bin. You had to use a kerosene lamp just like in the country. This place had a vintage stove and an old wooden icebox that needed blocks of ice.

In the summer, we tried to afford the ice for the wooden box, which was filled every day. The friendly iceman would chop ice into a twenty-five or fifty-pound piece. He would carry it up three flights of stairs on his back with tongs. He would then place it in our wooden icebox that had a pan underneath it that collected the water drippings. This pan needed emptying and invariably overflowed at least twice a day. The poor tenant below would have to endure the hardship.

This same man came around in the winter and sold us coal for our little potbelly stove. The ash from the potbelly stove would need to be removed properly and then carried out and dumped on the pavement below. The ash waste kept the sidewalks from being slippery during the winter months. Then one would revisit the cold, unheated halls in order to retrieve more coal from your personalized, padlocked bin, which came as an extra and was assigned to each tenant.

These cold water flats were drafty deep freezers. A public toilet was located in the hall and used by all tenants, according to their floors. The occupants who used these common indoor conveniences sometimes displayed a vulgar sloppiness, which greatly perturbed me. I could not believe their utter contempt for the next in line.

Our flat was located close enough to the bathroom as well as the coal bin. The light bulb was positioned in the hallway just outside our door. Our only furnishings were a table and a few chairs along with two chamber beds built into the wall.

Ah, the chamber beds...a bed of sorts that would fold into the wall. You would see this unique invention in old movies. The funny side of this kind of bed was that it was always popping out of the wall and falling on someone's unsuspecting head. But the unfunny side, which was unspoken and concerning, was the unmistakable bedbugs. These tenacious tenants of Chicago, creatures of villainous breeding, roamed deep in the guts of structures. Not even country life could be equated with this type of pest; the bedbug was usually a city dweller. In the country, the bugs stayed where they belonged, outside.

Now, don't get me wrong; these wall beds were never made for bugs. It's highly probable, that under ordinary circumstances, this would be a very compact and convenient modern necessity, especially where space is at a premium. But, in the '30s and '40s, these beds trapped these tiny creatures inside the walls, where they became nasty tenants with an invitation to a blood fest.

Often I would wake up to find Mother standing over me with a lamp in hand trying to pick the nasty things from my face and body. Waking up to the feeling of your skin virtually crawling all over with bedbugs was something you don't ever forget.

In frantic panic, I would swat at my body to rid myself of these bloodthirsty bugs. Then I would help pick them off of my younger brother and sisters, who were fast asleep in their innocence. They would literally eat us up and leave large welts on us. Mother would apply the only medication we could afford. It was baking soda.

Mother would not have looked normal without the old faithful insect spray gun in hand. She constantly aimed at some corner or nook, where a contemptible insect was campaigning. The insecticides we used were very real and came in only one fragrance. It was guaranteed to cross your eyes and make them red, or turn you ghost white, or even a beautiful complexion of blue. If you got it on you, it was truly a patriotic way to go, for your medal of honor was there for many days. We were living in a nightmare.

The bed bugs weren't the only problem with these terrible places. Our situation was getting worse all the time. Our place was so bad, especially with the cold weather, that it was most unbearable. During the day it was extremely cold, and at night you could literally see vapors blowing into the cups of your hands, that could be seen from across the room by lamp light. We never had any proper clothes for either indoors or outdoors. With holes in our underwear and shabby clothing on our backs, we were a sad looking bunch.

A year went by, and we endured never-ending sickness like plagues. We always needed to attend a clinic, where we stood in line from early morning on. We seldom got attended to before noon. Mother would lose a full day's work. We would get up early, before the sun came up, and head out on foot for the long journey to the clinic. You were lucky if you were first in line and got through all the preliminaries before the mad rush. We would wait in line as we passed through one department into the next, being processed until we finally got to the proper floor. This process was tedious and slow. You had to move from one seat to the next. By the time you were passed from one desk to the next, they had a mile-long record of information.

I felt like a celebrity, as I was interviewed by each and every caseworker, giving all the details. When we reached the children's department, we did an hours' worth of busy work on the blackboard, while we waited patiently for our kidneys to produce enough fresh specimen.

Then my turn came, and I was required to go into the little booth with the white curtain. A strange man in a white coat came in and peeked under the paper at my body parts. I was experiencing a complete examination. It was something that I had not been informed about. I was humiliated, invaded by fingers, fingers, fingers, until I thought I would die. After that, I no longer felt I had any privates, privates, privates.

These smart fellows seemed a wee bit mixed up. They would look down my throat if I was constipated and examine my buttocks when my throat was sore. The small paper sheet used to cover oneself was a joke. It provided little if no covering at all. I knew the minute a white-coated gentleman entered the booth it was going to be everything goes. Through all this poking and prodding, we managed to give the interns lots of knowledge.

After spending an entire day in the clinic, you were dismissed with a little bottle of pills in a variety of sizes and colors. Directions were to take two green and one red if it was your head, and one green and two red if it was your feet.

Father always said, "Just leave it alone. It's all in your head." Mother said, "Some things are not in your head," but believed that a good dose of onion tea or castor oil would take care of what ails you.

These lengthy clinic visits included being tested for glasses and having our teeth examined. This is how my poor vision diagnosis was discovered. Mother was not able to afford glasses for me, so my teacher, who knew about my astigmatism, offered me a seat in the front of the class.

By attending school, we were provided with the school's lunch program, on which we survived. Sometimes, we went to school without food in our bellies, and the soup and Jell-O the school provided wasn't enough to keep me from fainting at the blackboard. Sometimes, we attended school even if we were sick. With our continuous whooping cough-like symptoms, we were hoisted into the hallways for disturbing the peace. We went through many a case of winter bronchitis in the hall. Mother would try her best to doctor us at home with garlic and other home remedies. Nothing seemed to work.

Our health issues were never-ending. Velma started getting migraine headaches, and Juanita looked emaciated with her skeleton shape. We were not alone in our dilemma. The streets were full of sick and half-starved individuals.

Our situation worsened each day. Then out of the blue, Father knocked at the door. He had his new invention in hand. It was the Portable Sanitary Milking Machine. He explained that he had applied for a patent. He said he had kept a promise to Mr.

Keyser that he made several years back. The patent was dated April 4, 1936, Patent pending.

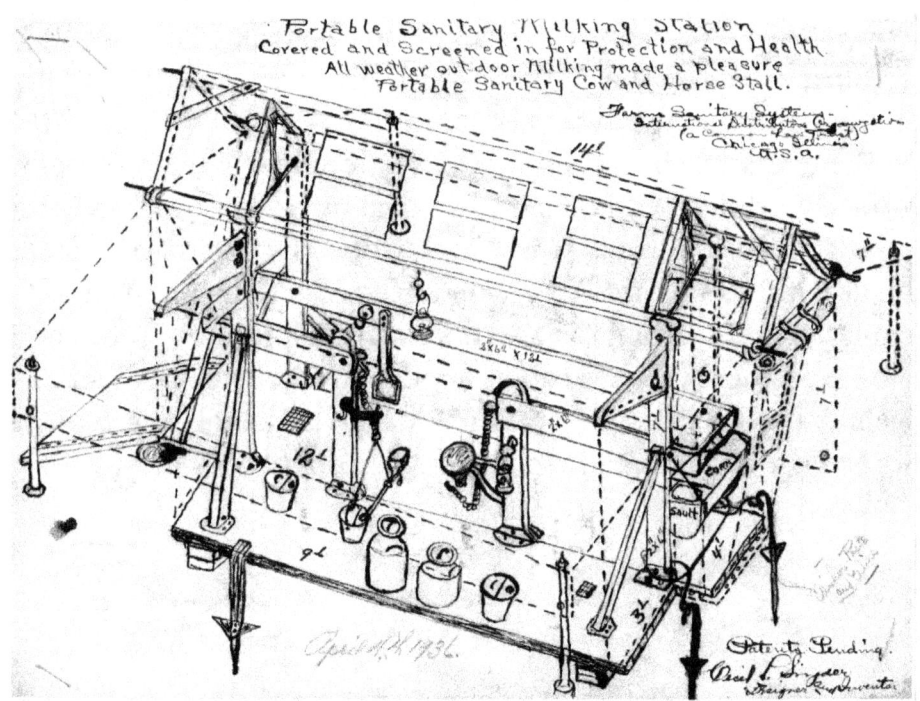

Portable Sanitary Milking Machine

Mother was displeased and didn't want to hear any details. She was tired of the same old, same old, and stated, "The gall of that man." She sincerely felt he had taken leave of his senses to even suggest such a thing as a new patent, a new invention. "On top of all we are going through with hunger and being destitute, your father's utter nonsense is foolish. He is lacking sound judgment." Father was bearing a white flag, and he was waving it up high. "Tell your father to plunge into a new duty. Get a job," she ordered from on high from our tenement window.

In a way, Father was trying so hard, in the only way he knew how, to recapture Mother's admiration. To us kids he was truly great, and we looked forward, with great anticipation, to his faithful and frequent mini visitations.

Father's visits became routine. We would meet on the corner. One day, while visiting outside, several birds flew overhead and one dropped some doo on my forehead. As I stood there looking up at Father's face intently, Velma started to laugh hysterically, while Junior's response was, "It's a sign of a spot of good luck." However, there was no visible connection with lady luck, as Lady Delilah had predicted. To me luck was no lady at all. Instead she was a fleeting manhandling maverick, a double dealer.

CHAPTER 25

A State Of Constant Flux

Our life was cruel and harsh, and Mother felt she had no alternatives. I was worried about Mother. I thought she was going to give up the ghost and die. She would say at times, "It all just seems so futile." Life was all work and scrub, scrub, scrub. With overflowing pans of water under a wooden icebox, if you were fortunate enough to have one, a peeling oilcloth smeared with peanut butter on the kitchen table, and a bathtub full of soiled clothes which were rubbed and scrubbed by hand, that was all that life was about.

Mother certainly didn't have much to look forward to, with the cries of hungry children begging for a bite, and a pantry that was always bare, with maybe a bone for soup. With four youngsters in one bed, two with weak kidneys, and bedbugs lounging in a feller's ear every night, it was becoming a dreadful way of life.

I once asked Mother, "Why don't we go back to the farm?"

Her reply was, "I can't get enough money together for train fare, and we surely can't walk that far." It was plain and simple; our tickets were punched and the trip into the mad full circle of the Depression was gaining speed and momentum.

With Roosevelt in power for years, the poor suffered. I remember my mother standing on a corner outside a store one day with a neighbor, listening to the radio. Not too many people could afford radios. The first lady of the land, Mrs. Eleanor Roosevelt, was advising housewives on the economics of stretching a budget without waste. In Mrs. Roosevelt's best squeaky voice and well-intentioned manner, she was giving the recipe for drying coffee grounds and tea leaves in order to use them several times. There were no words to describe how a suggestion such as this was received, especially when hardly anyone had even a nickel for a cup of coffee. She was clueless. How could she not know the state of the economy? Her comment was quite offensive.

Many people had no home. They erected makeshift shelters in vacant lots and along the streets. The breadlines were long, and men were knocking on any door for a morsel of food. The cockroaches ran down plastered walls; leaky toilets constantly ran over and spilled; it was a way of life. If you were lucky enough to have a place with steam heat, you had a luxury apartment for sure. These privileges were few and far between. With such gross inequities ever present, the suffering of humanity was immense.

Jobs were virtually nonexistent. I myself tried to get a job, but no help was needed, and the majority of people who did need help could not pay. One tavern owner on the west side hired me to scrub floors and take care of two little children. I worked like a dog from Friday night until Sunday night, and all I received was my meals and fifty cents for the weekend. Then summer rolled around, and I started working as a full-time twenty-four-hour mother's helper. For my efforts, I received three dollars a week. It was undeniably the low wages that hindered the poor.

In July 1938, Father came around and told us that he was going to Washington D.C. and would see us upon his return. I would not know for many years, until after the death of my father, what exactly it was that he was doing in Washington D.C. The newspaper article dated July 18, 1938, from the *Chicago Daily* would describe him as an employee of the Attorney General's Department working for General Gordon Conant. He was working on an inquest surrounding the death of Mabelle Horlick Sidley, the malted milk heiress. There was some mystery surrounding her death and the facts in the possession of the government were presented at the inquest by Cecil L. Snyder.

Later in that same year, a court case concerning Father with the Welfare Department was approaching. Mother knew that the Welfare Department was planning on sending Father to the Cook County's Psychopathic Hospital. Mother, in her desperation, took Father to court for child support. The state stepped in and tried with all their might to prove him insane and have him committed. The story hit the front page of the *Chicago Tribune*. The head of the Psychopathic Hospital tried to prove him insane. The verdict was given, and even Judge Albert Isley was impressed with Mr. Snyder's abilities. Quoting the papers, "When Mr. Snyder, who styles himself as an inventor, won his release in court from the Psychopathic Hospital by habeas corpus proceedings, the first thing he did was to rise and defend himself, with all the evidence in against him, he rose and fired his lawyer in the open court, and then acted as his own proper attorney, and explained his plan to sue the states, and thereby convinced the jury and the judge that he was perfectly sane." He had put those doctors in their place.

Mother had failed at her forced attempt to have him committed, but the Welfare Department assured her they would nail him the next time. I was so worried about my father. The way things were going I could hardly concentrate on my schoolwork. I feared what was going to happen to him. In my lack-of-concentration moods, I wound up falling down the school stairs breaking my leg and my foot. I was laid up for a long time. Mother said I was careless.

When I graduated from grammar school, our financial status was absolutely nil allowing for no funds for any dress or shoes for my graduation. I had to participate whether or not we could afford the necessities. A friend of Mother's, who Mother worked for, offered to help out in the purchase of my dress and shoes. This allowed me the good fortune to be able to graduate in a decent dress. This kind lady gave me my first Bible as a graduation present and let me work in her small shop to pay for my graduation picture. The good Lord provided for this little sparrow.

Next door to the Franklin Grammar School was Waller High School, which is where I attended my freshman year of schooling. Most of my friends were in about the same financial position as our family and lived as I did, in some of the worst kind of poverty. Strangely enough, the poor still remain housed in these locations, as they were many years ago.

INVENTOR ANONYMOUS

Eleanor's 8th grade graduation picture

CHAPTER 26

Juvi Nightmare

I was in my first year in high school when Velma disappeared. Mother was desperately trying to feed us and pay the rent. She was having extreme difficulty. She felt she could no longer take care of us and made a decision to turn us over to the state.

Without warning, one morning around the noon hour, a paddy wagon pulled up. A small woman about forty-five years old stepped onto the pavement and came to our door. At first I believed she had the wrong address, but Mother invited her into our flat. They talked quietly and then the woman requested I put on a sweater and come with her. My sister was missing, and of course I knew my mother was very worried. However, I knew nothing about her whereabouts or why she was gone. Velma had not mentioned to me any plans for running away, and I was not too familiar with any of her close girlfriends.

I asked no questions and in sincere faith, I was obedient. It was then that I realized I was being taken to the paddy wagon. I was placed in the back on a bench-like seat along the wall. The woman got in and sat down beside me. The wagon began to roll away, and I became curious, asking, "Where are you taking me?" Immediately her manner changed. She was no longer quiet and calm. As she moved closer to me on the seat, she barked, "Never mind young lady, you just sit quietly on that seat and don't try anything funny. You don't want be handcuffed now do you?" My heart pounded. *What is she saying? I must be hearing things. She must have made some kind of terrible mistake. This cannot be happening. I am not a criminal.* My thoughts raced wildly through my head, and my emotions were all mixed and stirred. I had no idea what was wrong. *Why am I being taken away from home? Where are we headed?*

My sister's name was not mentioned in the paddy wagon, so I did not correlate her misadventure with what was happening in the present. I could not even think straight. Usually I was a calm person, but somehow I had turned this woman's manner into sudden toughness toward me. I kept turning thoughts over in my mind. *Why would she say not to try anything funny? Is she really afraid I'm going to do something? What would I do anyway?* I was told to remain quiet. No further information was given. I was emotionally confused and could not unravel any details.

After what seemed like forever, we pulled into the driveway of a huge stone or brick building. I could not see very well from the tiny window of this miserable wagon. I had never in my life been inside one of these vehicles, although I had many times seen them in front of taverns where I lived. It was frightening as well as degrading.

When the officer who was in the front cab stopped the wagon, he got out and came to the rear door, which was obviously bolted shut. The two doors swung open. He grabbed me by my arm rather roughly, and with a firm grip he pulled me to the ground. I almost slipped getting out of the wagon, the steps were so narrow. With the two of them flanking my side, and taking a firm grasp on both my arms, they hauled me toward the building and actually pushed me inside the door. Without a word of explanation, I was shoved into a room with bars on the doors and told to sit down or they would handcuff me. I just sat there numb and dumb. I couldn't make a bit of sense out of the situation. All I saw were people rushing around the room, and one woman who never took her eye off me, not even for a minute.

From there I was taken into an examination room and told to remove my undergarments and get on the table. A man in a white coat came into the room and told me to spread my legs for a smear test. I had no idea what they were going to do, and I refused to allow them to touch me. I began to cry for my mother, and they told me it was no use shedding tears; it was too late. I became horrified. *My word, what did they mean? What have I done? I must be dreaming. This must be a bad dream.*

No, it was not a bad dream. I was experiencing the wildest and most severe disgraceful incident of my life. They forced me to lie on a table while they put an instrument inside me. A woman stood there and helped hold me down. After a humiliating examination, they told me not to worry. That was the understatement of the century. I was in shock and frightened beyond my wildest dreams. I was fourteen years old and alone without recourse. I was told to get dressed. I was then taken into a different room. There, I was properly seated. My arm was then hooked up to a machine. Immediately I knew this was a lie detector, for my father had spoken of this machine many times in connection with the Lindbergh case. I was asked many crazy questions, which I tried to answer as best I could. I was so upset from the examination in the other room that all I could do was sob.

After a while, the test was over. They released me to the same woman who brought me there. She took me across the courtyard to another building. I was then taken to another room, where they told me to remove my clothes again. I started to scream, and they told me to shut up or they would take me to the lockup. A woman in a blue uniform came in and handed me a heavily starched uniform with large pockets and told me to remove the cross on my neck. I refused to do this for this was my very own cross, and it meant the world to me. She then proceeded to rip it from my neck. "You can't have things like that in here," she firmly informed me. My thoughts raced. *In here, where's in here?* I inquired, "Where am I?"

"You mean you don't know where you are, girl? You seem worried."

I thought, *this can't be jail, I can't be in jail. They got something all wrong. Why am I in jail?* I then answered, "I don't know where I am or why I'm here, and I want to go home."

"Well, you're not going home for a while. This is the receiving floor of the juvenile home. You must know why you're here. What are you trying to kid me about? You girls are all alike, pretending that you don't know. You know. You're not dumb," she went on.

It was no use. I could not find out anything and could not convince her that I didn't know why I was there. Well, I was there for almost a week. I was placed on a scrub team. I scrubbed the halls twice a day and cleaned the toilets. During this time, I got acquainted with a couple of other girls and we talked. One was in for running away. The other had been caught in the act of stealing from a downtown store. There were several others who were there for different reasons, but I can't remember what they had done.

After a week, I was well aware of where I was. However, no one would discuss my problem, and I could not find answers. I guess I remained in a state of shock for two weeks, just going through the motions of eating and sleeping, like in a strange fog. Whenever I was handed a bucket and told to fill it up and take the hall, I knew exactly what they meant. I would scrub and scrub each day thinking about what it all meant.

Finally, one day, I was told that I was being transferred to the second floor, for my quarantine was over. Once there, I was told to put on a green uniform, which identified me to the second floor. This floor seemed different, for there was a small recreation room and a matron in attendance who wore a white uniform. The atmosphere was somewhat more unhurried, and I began to relax and settle back into consciousness.

On Sundays, we went to church according to our religion. I was Protestant and went to services designated for Protestants. During the week, we did chores on the floor according to assignment. There were beds to make and kitchen work to do. It was a completely new way of life, looking out windows that had bars on them.

I was beginning to realize that I was a captive. I could not understand why no one was telling me about my case. This word "case" was a new expression for which I needed to become accustomed to hearing. Everyone always referred to "their case." I seemed to be the only one that was overly curious about my case and quizzed the matrons. They would just listen but refuse to talk. They said it was against the rules to discuss cases. Although I tried to convince them I had no case, they assured me that I had one.

I began to wonder about Mother, because on visiting day no one would come. I began to think that maybe I was in here because of what Velma had done. I tried to think about where that scamp had gone and why. I wondered if they found her, then maybe I would be released. I had so many unanswered questions, and no one would answer them.

I was given a written IQ test and asked if I wanted to attend school. This news was a bit of happiness, for I thought I was going home. Nothing could have been further from the truth. School was right across the courtyard within the walls that you could not see over. This little school building was quite similar to the little schoolhouse that I had attended in the country. Attending class there was not the same. I could not concentrate. My mind would wander. I would peer at the high wall, watching the snow fall, as winter was starting to consume the earth.

Everything became routine, with the weeks rolling into months. Finally, Mother came one day to see me. We visited in the dining room of the second floor. Our visit was a shambles. She questioned me about my sister who she claimed was still missing, possibly dead or in a white slavery ring, as she put it. I asked her to take me home, and she told me there was no home.

"What do you mean there is no more home?" I blurted out. "What happened?" I started to cry. Mother seemed like a stranger, someone I did not know.

"There is no home. I could not take any more hardship," she informed me sadly.

"But, mother, what about me? What about me?" I implored. Mother had no answers, and I became unruly in my confusion. I screamed for her to take me home. I had done nothing wrong. It all fell on deaf ears. She had made her mind up, and that was that.

"You belong to the state now. The way things are, you will have to be a ward of the state until you're eighteen years old," she said with finality.

"You mean I'm never going to get out of here? You don't mean that Mother, you can't mean that." I was desperate for an answer. When this bit of information was made known to me, I began to get hysterical. Mother was told by the matron to leave, that I'd be all right later. Mother got up and left. As she passed through the door, she didn't even turn to say goodbye.

I yelled in her direction, "Don't ever come and see me again. I hate you for what you've done to me. I'm innocent. I want out. I hate this place." My heart sank. *Oh dear God, please don't make this terrible nightmare be true.* But, sadly it was true. I was locked up for no reason at all and must remain until I turned eighteen, which seemed like such a long way off.

It was a whole lifetime to me, and I could no longer see my friends. I thought of the wonderful boy who lived down the street, the one who went past my house on the way to the beach many times whistling a Marine song. We had never kissed, but I knew he liked me. Then there was another boy who had bought me roses when I graduated, with money he had earned himself. His mother accompanied him to deliver them to my door with a special card to match the roses. I thought about how sweet it was for him to do that especially when the poor had so little money. I thought of how long he must have worked to save the money for the flowers, the very first flowers I ever received in my whole life. I'll never forget the day he came to my house with his mother. I had only seen this boy, Johnny, once or twice. He was the epitome of shyness. I could not have been more surprised in my embarrassment. However, Mother did not take the same view and was quietly suspicious of this young man, who so boldly brought his mother along, just to bring me flowers.

Then, I wondered, what would people think about my disappearance from the neighborhood? No one, not even I, could have ever imagined such an extreme happening. What would my girlfriends think? Would they even know? Then, I thought of Father and wondered if possibly Velma had gone with him somewhere. I knew not how to figure this new situation. All I could do was to wait and see.

I began to bide my time and fall into line with the work. The months passed, and soon the spirit of Christmas began to seep under the doors of this place called "the Juvenile." A tree went up in the recreation room. All at once, a new glow was cast upon a pretty depressed girl.

As time ticked on, I became a permanent fixture. The matrons all liked me because I did my work without any trouble. Compliments began to fly to and fro between the matrons about my good behavior and good work. I was then recommended for private dining room duty. Through the grapevine, I had been cued-in to the fact that this was the most exceptional privilege given only to the most highly recommended girls. It was rumored that if one got private dining duties, one got better food. Now I was used to some pretty awful food from a meager supply at home, being hungry most of the time anyway, but I was looking forward to better food. The slop they usually served us here was mostly watered-down, overcooked dishes with much grease. I was always sick to my stomach. I knew that private dining duty meant you would eat better. I looked forward to this change. The opening was available and I took the plunge. I was not disappointed in the least.

This transition required a handoff to a new caretaker, a short lady with owl-like glasses perched on the end of her nose. We were known as her trustees. She was like a mother duck with a quaint waddle. She had large keys, on a huge round ring, which hung at her side. It made her look important. As trustees, each morning at ten o'clock we would carry soaps and cleaners, a mop and a carpet sweeper across the grounds to the other building, all without any guards or handcuffs. We girls would follow behind her, as we were headed off to clean the interior of the doctors' bachelor apartments. We scrubbed bathrooms and vacuumed the front areas and made ready the front for the dinner hour.

After the dinner hour, we were allowed to eat the food that the doctors left over in the serving bowls on the table. We then would clear the table and do the dishes. I enjoyed this new position and the chores, for it was an outlet that released my mind's confinement. I got a better grade of food and enjoyed a greater freedom than the majority of the other girls. I had the caretaker's trust. Not once did she ever have to mention disciplinary measures toward me or warn me about running away. Her trust in me made me feel grand, and soon I became well-liked and learned to loosen up a bit.

The privileges and extra comfort I received were not favors granted; they were earned because of my good behavior and because of my long stay with the home. I had been there close to a year, and time began to fly by. As a youth, I began to deal with my terrible confinement. I knew all the matrons by their names, and they seemed to sympathize with my personal problems. At times, one would confide assurances to me that I would be handled fairly since they were aware that my case was surely different.

I saw many girls come and go. While there, I saw some of the strangest things happen. Some pretty bad eggs caused a bit of trouble. It seemed that most of the trouble went on at night. Several times we were rousted from our beds to march before the night matron. She was a real tough cookie. She would stand for no nonsense. The girls all hated her, so they would flood the washrooms with water at night by stuffing old rags down the toilet bowl. They would conceal things between their legs and hide them in places like under their mattresses in their dormitories. One night a girl ripped up sheets during a commotion of high tension. I couldn't keep up with all the things that were contrived by these girls, for I was busy with thoughts of home and Father and the rest of the family. When I went to bed at night, I said my prayers and usually cried myself to sleep from all the emptiness inside me.

One day, while I was sitting quietly in the recreation room, a burly matron came in. We were sewing a brassiere, which was a project that had been initiated for the girls. We were just getting big enough to really need this type of garment, and I had never owned a bra. The matron announced, "Snyder is there a Snyder girl here?"

"Yes, ma'am," I quickly answered.

"Come with me. You are wanted at the main building," she informed. *Could it be I'm going home? Oh thank God. Maybe they found Velma. Maybe this thing will finally be all over.* I felt a surge of hope in my heart which nearly jumped out of my chest. I tossed aside the material I was sewing and rushed after the matron, who was already on her way to the stairs. After a few words of caution, she informed me that I would not need to change my clothes. At this point, I froze. *Maybe I'm wrong. Maybe I'm not going home. Maybe I'm going for more tests and questions*. Whatever was taking place, I needed to follow her to the other building across the courtyard.

Nearing the building, I spotted that same juvenile officer in the same black dress and hat, just like it was yesterday in the paddy wagon. She was waiting at the door. Her musk perfume curled my nose. "I hear you've been a good girl," were her words of greeting. I nodded my head yes. "Well, I suppose I can trust you today. Your trustee tells me...," she blabbed on and on, but I didn't hear the rest of what she said, for I was too busy noticing her legs; she had one shorter than the other. I had not seen this when we first met. She appeared crippled. I almost felt sorry for her for a moment, but then I remembered how changeable she could be, nice one minute and forceful the next.

I thought back to the first day when she brought me here and the sneaky way I was taken into custody. I thought about what they had done to me in the examining room with that terrible instrument and the light under the sheet. I couldn't feel any compassion for her. She seemed evil to me. Without expression or words, I followed along as she halfway clung to me, sort of in a guiding fashion. We went up the elevator and entered through a door which had big bold letters on it, reading, *Judge Black*. She gently pushed me into the room.

It was a small room with a bench along the wall. I could see it was a tiny courtroom. Seated on the bench was my mother. I spotted her first. She looked flushed, tight lipped and dismal. I did not especially like the look she gave me when I entered. A man was sitting close to the door and not too close to Mother. He was a Filipino youth about age twenty-two, and quite handsome. I did not recognize him. Sitting next to my mother was a girl who seemed vaguely familiar, but I could not rightly give her face a name.

My sudden surveillance of the situation was one of curiosity. I was told to be seated, and no words were exchanged. The matron who brought me in limped over to Mother and leaned down and whispered a few words. She then returned to my side without so much as a look or an ounce of emotion. She was stiff, stodgy, and precise.

After a few minutes, the bailiff came into the room with some books and papers. We were asked to stand as the judge came into the room. We rose from our seats and the mallet came down, startling me. "This court will come to order, the case of Snyder versus???????, is now in session." I could not understand the name that was announced after our name. It was a long foreign one, and it just fluttered over my head.

I was told to come forward. As I stood before the judge, I was told to place my hand on the Bible and swear to tell the truth. After several simple questions, such as name and so forth, I looked up at this judge who didn't seem to see me. He was busy talking and looking down at papers. Then the girl who was sitting next to Mother came forward at the judge's request. She began to answer questions as though she knew my family, especially my sister. I listened intently and suddenly, as if a fog had lifted, I realized that she was saying things about my sister that I could not believe. There she was standing before the judge telling some of the most bold-faced lies I've ever heard. I began to slowly place where I had seen her face. Of course, she was a neighbor from a nearby street, but I couldn't quite remember just where. She was certainly not any friend of mine, and she talked like she knew Velma, but the things she was saying just had no rhyme or reason.

Well, I stood as long as I could and listened to her story. As it got progressively worse, I felt steam building up inside of me. Before I realized it, I started screaming, "Liar, Liar" right to her face and punched her right smack dab in the kisser. The woman juvenile officer rushed to help the girl who was screaming for help. I guess I lost control, and before I knew it, I had knocked her to the floor. We were then separated at once.

The judge rose like a mechanized statue, with his black robe hanging from his arm, his outstretched finger pointing directly in my direction, "Blackstone, Blackstone," he yelled at the top of his voice. "Put that one in Blackstone. Take her away."

I remember little of what happened next, but everybody was rushing around. I was being dragged by the nape of my neck out the door and down the hall and across the courtyard to another building with a lady officer tugging at both my arms. I was in a daze. Before I realized it, I was back in the familiar first-floor receiving center. I was yanked down a hall at a high rate of speed, so much so that I could hardly keep up. I muttered, "Stop it," but this did not prevent her from dragging me toward the end of the hall where the scrub buckets were kept. There, a big iron door swung open and revealed two cells of confinement, tiny 4' x 6' compartments. Both were narrow and contained only a bed hanging from the wall on a chain. The bars on the doors were exactly the same as the ones on Father's cell, only now, I would be the one looking out bars.

I was told to remove my shoes and hairpins, and that I would be here for two weeks on bread and water. This was my punishment for being "incorrigible." This word I had not heard before and was worried that something was wrong with me. I could not understand the whole picture. It all happened so fast. I could not catch up with the merry-go-round.

As I tried to climb on the bed, which was way too high for me, I began to realize that I was going to have a lot of time to think, having to stay in here for two weeks. I was completely confined. No reading was allowed. No loose articles were permitted, not even a comb. When I needed to use the toilet, I had to bang on the walls with my fists or call out.

One matron, who was compassionate toward me, kept me from going insane. She would slip me an apple once in a while. She knew I had been a private dinner room helper, but she felt I had acted irrationally in the judge's courtroom. After explaining the whole story to her, she felt that a grave mistake had taken place. I would remain in this cell completely alone. The other cell next to mine was empty.

As I lay on my bed, I had many hours to turn the whole matter over in my mind. The more I thought about it, the more I realized that I would have done the same thing all over again. That girl, whoever she was, had evidently been prompted to speak the way she did and make up lies. She convinced the judge that both Velma and I deserved to be put away. In my confinement, I started talking to myself just like Mother had done. I passed the time away singing songs and reciting Bible verses. Then finally, the day arrived for my removal. I was sent back to the second floor, where some of the girls I knew had gone home.

The next few days, I found out that my sister, Velma, was now also placed in this institution. They had placed her on a floor above me. These girls wore gray uniforms and were mostly older or married. Or, as the grapevine had it, they were non-virgins. I couldn't believe my sister was up there. I requested permission to see her, and of course this request was denied.

One matron, a devout Christian, knew my whole story and what had happened to me. She said it was the most grave injustice she had seen in many a day. She worked out a plan for me to see my sister for a few minutes in the upstairs gym, only because she thought it was a sin to keep two sisters separated.

Velma and I visited for only a few minutes, but I got to find out some important things that filled in some of the missing pieces. I asked her about Juanita and brother Vern, Cecil Junior. She did not know one single thing. She said she had run off and gotten married because she was tired of living the way we were, and that she loved the boy. She told me of how they had been arrested by the police across the state line and that her husband was jailed with charges of the "Man Act." I was not familiar with this term. I only knew that jail meant they had locked him up too.

My sister had not seen the family or Mother and didn't know where Father was. I was not too much better off than before, but at least I had a chance to talk to my sister. I was thankful to this kind matron's arrangement for the chance to see my sister. I did not see Velma again.

The next visiting day, Mrs. Honer, an acquaintance from the past, came to see me. She tried to explain our situation and said Mother was pretty bitter and that Mother had a complete breakdown. She said that my sister, Juanita, had been taken to Ridge Farm because she was so run down and thin, and that my brother, Vern, had been sent to Glenwood Home for Boys. Mrs. Honer explained that the judge had recommended that Velma and I be sent to Geneva. This was the reason that Mrs. Honer was so concerned. She could not see two fine girls, as she put it, get sent to a girls' prison for absolutely nothing and spend the rest of their lives with a record. She said, "Eleanor I will do everything in my power to get this Judge Black to change his mind, but after you punched that girl the way you did, he thinks you should serve his sentence."

Well, Mrs. Honer was right. I suppose that was an unkind act I engaged in against that girl, but I could not and would not admit complete sorrow for it. I had acted on principle, and my principles had turned out to be troublesome for me. The girl was lying and that was that. I was a helpless victim, as was my sister. Mrs. Honer was also worried about my mother, for she had completely changed and was very bitter. With Mrs. Honer's assurance, she told me she would get the church to help. She told me to pray hard and ask God for help, for the family was in a terrible mess. Then Mrs. Honer left. I would not see her again until almost seven years later.

CHAPTER 27

Convent

Springtime came and the snow was beginning to melt. I was still peering through the windows with bars on them. It was a gloomy time. I had only seen my mother those two times and Mrs. Honer and my sister once. I was beginning to feel forgotten and desperately lonely.

Then one day, a car came for Velma and me. We were mysteriously zipped away from the jail where I had spent over a year. I wondered what my future would be. My sister and I were reunited in the car, but we were not allowed to talk. After a long ride, we arrived at the doors of another institution. A nun with a long black habit met us at the door. Neither of us could have known what they had planned for us. The nun talked softly, as she helped us get acquainted with our new surroundings. She said this place was called a convent and that visitors were permitted once a month. She seemed to know about our circumstances but refused to give us any details about the whys and wherefores.

"I know, child," she said, "life is cruel. We must ask God to help us. This will be your home now, until you are old enough to be released from the custody of the State of Illinois. You will be given a class name. No one will ask you your business. You are not to discuss this matter with anyone. The class name will conceal your identity. All girls are in here for different reasons. We don't discuss these reasons at any time. You will learn the rules and obey, or you will be punished. There will be no rebellion. You will learn to live with your situation as best you can; just ask God to help. He will answer your prayers."

I recognized we had traded bars for another form of confinement, the convent.

I became Mary Catherine and Velma became Gemma. During our time in this convent we learned to love the nuns. Velma and I were separated. She was assigned to a different dormitory and a different recreational room than mine. Due to Velma's sickly condition, she was placed in the sewing room where she did crocheting. I was assigned to the laundry room, where I beat sheets. I was referred to as a sheet beater. I also scrubbed cement floors that were full of grease from the ugly, black, monstrous machines that operated the whole convent laundry.

I worked nine to ten hours a day. Many times, we were still not done in time for the supper hour. The deafening sounds from the steam presses and the machines with the huge tumblers made your ears pop. It was virtually impossible to hear anyone's conversation, even when they were yelling in your ear.

Talking was forbidden and only permitted during recreation. All other times we lived in silence, except in prayer. We prayed from morning until night. We sang one litany after the other, in a solemn response, in the form of supplication, and with great gusto, day in and day out, morning, noon and night.

In the first month I was there, I was required to have a once-a-week examination; they called it "the treatment." This continued for a solid month. A doctor did something to us with scissors and Mercurochrome and completed the treatment by stuffing cotton into our bodies. I wondered what they were doing to me. They would stick instruments inside my body, poking and clipping until I was so sore that when I got off the table, I could not walk. These mysterious treatments, that everyone got once a week, did not allow for even a nun to be allowed inside the room during the procedure. When inquiry or refusal was exhibited, you were told to lie down, close your mouth and open your legs, or you would be forced to submit.

I was just sixteen and never knew any sex life. I was horrified by this manhandling against my will. Being at the mercy of an institution and some quack doctor experimenting on young virgins and innocent girls is the most degrading kind of punishment and submission one could ever experience. I was just one victim among the many others, as I could not speak out.

With a month of confinement under my belt, I now qualified for my first visiting day. Wallace Keyser came to see me. He was given special permission. He carried an important message. The nun said he was allowed permission only because it was our first visit, and it was in place of Mother. Here was Wallace Keyser, our old friend, sitting before me. He looked so good and brought back such wonderful memories. I couldn't believe my tear-filled eyes. "It is so good to see you, Wallace. My, how you have grown," I said nervously.

After exchanging some old-time familiarities, the nun advised him to hurry with his message. Another shock was about to be unleashed. Wallace looked pale as he spoke, "Your father was arrested and given a quick trial and sent to the Elgin State Mental

Hospital for the insane." I saw his face going blurry before my eyes, as I fell back against the chair. When I came to my senses, the nun was holding my head up. I heard her say, "She'll be all right in a minute. She's just had a terrible shock."

When the blood flowed back into my face, I became hysterical and began to cry and scream. "No, no, not Father too. Oh dear God, what in the world is wrong with us? What have we done to deserve this terrible thing?" I became uncontrollable. "Don't leave, Wallace. Don't leave. We have no one, and nobody cares for us. Please, Wallace, tell my mother to come and get us. I want to go home." I cried my heart out, and finally the nun saw that I was beyond repair. Wallace seemed concerned but was helpless to do anything himself.

"She will come around," the nun said to Wallace. "All she needs is time."

Those words rang in my ears, and I became dead inside. I couldn't even pray. I went to mass in the morning like a zombie. During the day, I beat those sheets to a pulp. I beat and beat until I couldn't beat anymore. I was a commando beater. I swatted at those sheets until my guts hurt inside.

My sister didn't know about Father or Wallace's visit. I couldn't get up the courage to tell her. The poor thing was in the infirmary half the time with illness. The nuns said it was all in her mind, but it was her head. She had migraine headaches which were regular and severe. I didn't get to talk to Velma much. She seemed to have passed into fogginess and her tongue could find no words. She was in a world of her own and spent half her time in bed with her migraine spells.

Mother did not come to see us on visiting day. Each month flew by without a word. There was no correspondence. Then, many months later, a huge birthday cake came for me. It was placed at the table where I was assigned to eat. It was almost as big as the table. It was the first cake that I had ever received in my whole life. I couldn't believe it was for me. I knew Father was locked up and could not have sent it, even though I knew it was the kind of cake he might send. It certainly was gigantic in size, an absolute monster. When the nun called me in to see it, I couldn't believe my eyes.

"Are you sure this is for me?" I asked.

"Yes," Mother Superior replied. "It is for you, and it is from your dear mother."

Tears came into my eyes, as I looked at this huge birthday cake. "Your mother felt very bad about what has happened and wants to see you the next visit. She came a long way to see you." The nun was convincing enough. It had been a long time since I had seen Mother, and I had much time to think about my bitterness which overwhelmed me. My heart did soften a bit, and I did agree to visit with Mother the following month. I thanked the Mother Superior, and the girls all sang "Happy Birthday" to me. As I cut the cake and passed out pieces, I cried all over the thing with tears of joy.

That night, I lay in my clean, white bed in the dormitory and prayed for my father and my mother. I prayed for my sisters, Velma and Juanita and for my brother, who was out there somewhere, but I knew not where.

Then one morning, the nun called me over and told me that my sister, Juanita, was on the other side of the convent. A wall separated these two sides of the convent. We were never permitted to even look in that direction. It was against the rules. The nun said that once a week I could wave to her over the wall when we recreated outside, but we could not and would not be able to touch or speak to each other. It was strictly forbidden.

So, once a week I stood on the high stairway and waved to my little sister, Juanita. Oh how I waved. She seemed so near, but she was so far away. It was the most unbearable thing. I could not even begin to describe this awful feeling of separation.

Then on December 7, 1941, the day of the attack on Pearl Harbor, I was sitting on a recreational platform listening to an old-fashioned console radio. Dressed in a white veil and dress, I had just come from breakfast after being baptized for the third time. The nun turned on the radio, and we all were listening to the music when suddenly the program was interrupted by the President, whose announcement was loud and clear. Pearl Harbor was just attacked and war had been declared. Those words would forever be imprinted in my brain.

The day after the attack on Pearl Harbor, Velma and I were caught up in a week of solemn rituals. On December 8, we made our first Holy Communion. On December 9, we attended the Feast of the Immaculate Conception. On December 10, I made my confirmation. On December 14, Velma and I both became a child of Mary, Mother of God. We made new vows and together, with my sister at my side, we faced a completely new life.

My life became a prayerful one. I vowed that someday I would get out and I would tell the whole world what the government did to our family. I was finally released from the state, at the age of eighteen. Velma was released thirteen months after I was. Juanita would be released several years later. I did not see Vern until six or seven years after I was released.

CHAPTER 28

The Exodus

When I got out, Mother was living in Maywood right across the street from Proviso High School. She had obtained a job at the American Can Company working on a punch press. We shared a little tiny sleeping room, and I went back to high school. I learned that most of the schooling I had lost in the convent could not be made up easily. I was too old for school, but I returned anyway and gave it a good stab. While attending high school, I also worked nights at a little confectionery store on the corner. I served the high school crowd from Proviso.

Mother worked every day, and I worked every day and went to school. Mother saved her meager earnings to fund my education in a business college. She was attempting to make up for the schooling that I had lost in the confines of the state institution. I took a night course and graduated a year later, receiving a diploma.

Eleanor's college picture, age 22

It was many years later when I saw my father again, in the late '40s. He had come to Chicago looking for his family, who had been scattered to the winds because of the state-controlled split-up. I met him on the corner, for he did not want Mother to see him in his current condition. Father looked tired with his blind eyes and his old white cane. As we conversed, he spoke of tracking down Velma, who was living in a trailer court with two small babies. He somehow had located her through Mrs. Honer, who lived in Maywood. We spoke of Vern who had just recently been discharged from the Navy, not being married, and how he was no longer using the name Cecil Junior, due to the impact of bad publicity in the papers. Father still called him Sonny, for he was still Father's Sonny Boy.

I told Father what happened to us, and he cried out, "Oh! Dear God! I did not know what happened to you children. I searched everywhere, but your mother left no trace." Father wiped the tears streaming down his face with his handkerchief. As he stood there in front of me, I could clearly see his clothing was worn but immaculately clean. His shirt was faded and wrinkled.

Father explained how he was busy during the '30s and '40s, scrubbing floors and trying to get any job he could. You could tell that his skin was impacted from strong detergents of the scrub water. He said Vern had given him a little cash for bus fare back to Washington, but he wasn't going to take a penny more. Being destitute and nearly blind, he was still hoping that someday he would get to the Supreme Court for a decision. He apologized for not being able to have given us anything better and was sorry for the past sufferings we had experienced. His immortal cry was that dirty deal he had gotten from the legislature and how he looked forward to the day when he would bring in twenty-eight congressmen for a face-to-face confrontation. But sadly, Father was now following another beat, the tap, tap, tap, along the curb from a blind man's cane. He could no longer ride the bandwagon, engaging in legalities with the governmental bodies, or practice the art of a calligrapher creating plans or beautiful drawings.

After Father returned home, to Washington, D.C., Juanita, the youngest, had an opportunity to visit him. Her husband, a twenty-five-year man in the Marine Corps, was stationed out that way, so while passing through, she stopped in to see Father. Upon her return, Juanita said that Father was working for a small business, selling door to door. She said he was living just a few blocks from the White House in a room overrun with cockroaches. She said she straightened a picture on his wall and roaches scattered in all directions. She spoke of Father's mattress, which had seen better days, and how it was perched on top of two-pound coffee cans, and the place smelled of stale tobacco and unaired bedding. Mercifully, Father was almost blind and could not see his sorry plight. He made no excuses for his living conditions but seemed so happy to have Juanita, his baby girl, drop by to see him.

During the '50s I never got another chance to see him again, although I faithfully kept in touch with him through persistent correspondence. Throughout the years, I tried to keep his letters and papers safely in my possession, for the benefit of all the family, especially the grandchildren, who never got to meet their wonderful grandfather.

Most of his things were scattered and distributed among his friends, whom he trusted. When his faithful bookkeeper died in the late '40s, his widow delivered tons of letters and business ledgers to our house. Mother did not handle this situation well and burned everything, remarking that she was "not sorry." Father claimed, in many of his letters, that his residence was robbed and pilfered several times. Most of the papers he still had left in his possession were because he carried them on his person.

When Father died on February 13, 1963, he was broke, nearly blind and alone. His final resting place is unknown. No one ever heard of Cecil L. Snyder, the man who invented the Automobile Title Method. This is a terrible injustice. He was a great man and a great father, who remained hopeful for fifty years that the government would change their mind. My father was suing twenty-eight states and the federal government for patent infringement on his patent. Yes, it is true that the biggest patent monopoly in the world, the car title registration, belongs to the United States Government; and how did they acquire it? **Well, now you know**.

As for Mother, she continued to work in the American Can Company for twenty years making can tops. She lost her hearing from the noise of the cans rolling down the lines, day in and day out. Her fragile beauty only faded slightly, as she finally earned her retirement from the company at the age of sixty-five.

Minnie Snyder

With her circumstances as such, Mother did the best she could rearing us children. She deeply cared for Father, but her life was filled with much sorrow and despair. She was never able to completely understand him. In her words, she said he was "too deep" for her.

As for Mother and me, we forgave each other, for I sincerely loved both my parents. Her recollections of days with Father were summarized as "a frightening nightmare," for Father's promises of greatness revealed only that he existed in a fool's paradise. His dream became a living nightmare in his beloved America, with its constitutional rights for everyone. These rights, enshrouded in a rude awakening, were never a reality for him.

CHAPTER 29

Final Thoughts

It is most unbelievable, but sadly true, that one man could get involved in so many diversified, interesting and fatal happenings. It is hard to understand how one could have so much on the ball and such high principles, yet be so persecuted. One thing is for sure, he never bit the hand that bled him, yet all this remains deleted from the pages of time, as though he never existed.

When I reflect back, I ask myself where all those people who complimented my father on his monopoly were. Where were his fine friends, Henry Ford, who offered to buy my father's business, and John D. Rockefeller, who said, "Don't delay, get it while you can"?

On the strength of what my father already drew up in the past, my conviction is that he was a man beyond his time with predictions and ideas. He was an expert of design methods, law of mathematics, and calligraphy. He was an inventor with style. His drawings and inventions are clear. But as a lonesome inventor, a little grasshopper, he didn't stand a chance.

Even though he suffered absolute degradation, he was not a derelict. When asked how he felt about what happened to him, being put in a state mental hospital, he said, "I forgive them." If my father can forgive them, I must too. But in order to preserve the future, I must tell the world what happened, for the truth shall prevail no matter how long they try to suppress it. As poor as Father was, he would not substitute principles for money. He endured poverty and separation from his family without whimpering.

He was known as a man of great character and had a gentle manner with good breeding. He dressed like a gentleman in the '20s and '30s. He even presented himself with dignity in the '40s, with a faded, worn shirt on his back. In the face of hunger, loneliness and defeat, never once did he become violent or provoked to anger. His spirit was schooled to mildness by discipline and suffering. Not many can display these qualifications.

It was the Welfare Department that tore our family apart and governmental bodies that caused hardships. My father was dedicated to his life's work and struggled to get the states and the federal government to compensate him for the infringement of his patent and copyright. My mother was fully aware of his intentions and what he was trying to accomplish, but lost faith in his hopeful excuses, which carried him to the point of no return.

The policy of the Welfare Department and the law of the land was the direct reason for my father being committed to a mental hospital. My mother's plight was such that she felt she had no choice but to press charges for nonsupport. In desperation, she eventually gave us children over to the state. As wards of the state, we were placed in the hands of people without hearts. Words cannot describe state government-controlled institutions and their intentions. What they did to my sister and to me was only a sample of what goes on in these horrible places, to innocent people.

I know they say that what doesn't kill you makes you stronger, and life without surprise would be very dismal indeed, but there aren't any words to describe the horror of hunger and suffering that leaves scars forever in one's memory.

Putting people in state mental institutions or jails does not always solve the problem. Starving the people in the Great Depression was a good way to get rid of them, reducing them to animals. War also conveniently rids the masses of people. And, the doctors and lawyers all have work because of injustices. Freeing people from the confines of unjust laws which serve the rich and the politicians, must be done away with. Once the government is cleansed of the nefarious rats and given back to the people, our world can be better prepared to meet Christ and His new kingdom.

One lone man cannot compete with the rich and greedy, and my father was that man. The government with its political favor game should be played fairly, but it is not. Father was swallowed up in red tape. He was buried with governmental bombardments placed upon him, with restrictions and controls, which no one man could survive.

With each of us living in our own separate kinds of confinement, trying to make the best of things, Father too, was doing the same. During his stay in the mental hospital, he could have been of a vengeful mind. Instead he busied himself with plans and drawings, creating his perpetual waterpower plant. He said he invented this to help solve world problems. He handled his undeserving captivity in a manner befitting a genius, for it was important to him how he handled situations. Even though he endured difficulties his whole life, he was always looking to help someone. He gave with his ideas and his energy.

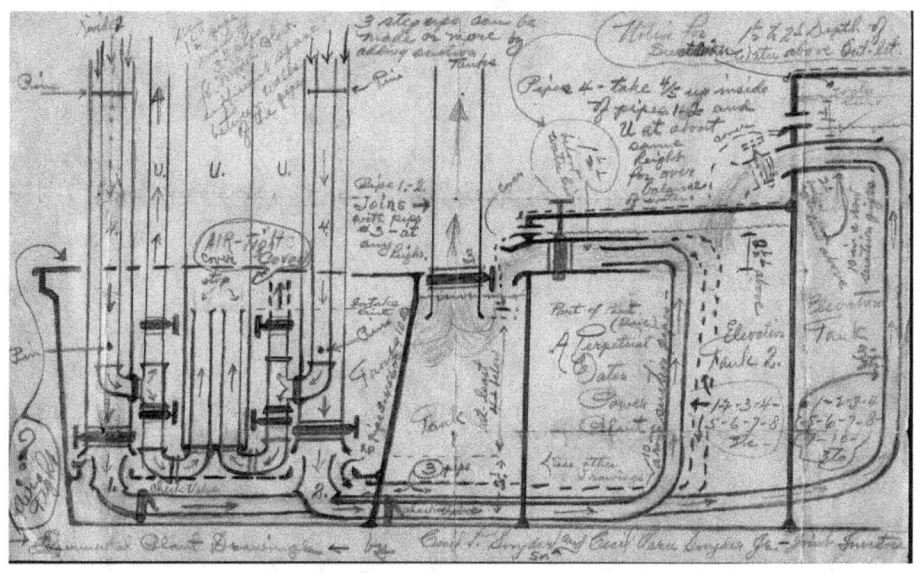

Perpetual Waterpower Plant, copyright 1944

I am deeply troubled when I think about our country, in a land so richly blessed. I cannot understand why the government would want to snatch away a man's livelihood. A man who only wanted to better people's lives. The government took away his rights and said they did it for the good of the people. They should have made restitution, but did they? There was never any recompense, no restitution whatsoever, just a *big fat zero*.

FINAL THOUGHTS

Stealing the rights from the Indian, the black man, the inventor shows an ugly head rearing in our government. Patting a man on the back for something worthwhile does no good when the other hand is stabbing him in the heart and removing his rights and property. What on earth is good about a piece of paper with constitutional rights on it if violations cause men to suffer?

One thing is for sure, my father's intentions were honorable. He certainly was not for politics or unjust laws or corruptness in any way. It is quite obvious that what he invented really benefited mankind and the government in no uncertain terms, and yet he never received any just compensation. Facts cannot be disputed. For his gifts to mankind, he received a lifetime of abuse and ridicule. In the eyes of God, one small man can be exalted while the greatest of governments can be crushed. *Beware history can repeat itself.*

Cecil L. Snyder did invent the system and the idea for the Abstract & Title for the automobile. It was patented and copyrighted, but the government stole it right out from underneath him. They got away with it successfully under sovereign immunity, reaping billions from his patent. He suffered deprivation of his intellectual property and was never compensated.

Inventors, who are the forgotten or unknown, fall by the wayside. The inventor, whose idea is great, is always at the mercy of someone who can steal and cheat it out from underneath them. In my father's case, it was the government. If the government had been honest, they would have compensated him and not tried to paint an ugly picture of his character. Instead, they enjoyed the fruits of his labor all served on a platter of legislature, who not only make the rules but can also break the rules.

My father's story is true. He was served à la carte side dishes, being jailed like a common criminal, over and over again. He then was deprived of his right to make a living, all served to him during the meal of his lifetime. And in the end, he had no decent burial.

Let me tell you right here and now, when we all stand in line for judgment, it is quite possible, when sifting and sorting through the souls, an interesting conversation between Jesus and Lucifer might be, "Here, you take two politicians, I'll take one inventor; You take three aldermen, I'll take one honest voter; For every half-dozen congressmen, I'll take one poor little taxpayer," and so on.

Remember God Is Watching All of Us

God alone with his wonderful eyes
peeps down through clouds and big blue skies.
Ever watching his flock of sheep
from the vigil of the devil who is never asleep.
Oh, heavenly Father, hear this prayer
and guide us with tenderness, and loving care.
We cry in darkness. Please hear and bless,
for this great green garden is in a terrible mess.
We are so tiny, and so very small
that our words seem insufficient to one so tall.
But, without your grace, or our daily bread,
our hungry minds would go unfed.
Great God, God of all that is good to say,
teach us to pray, and cast our demons far away.

By Eleanor Snyder

FINAL THOUGHTS

*Juanita and Velma seated, Eleanor standing
1972*

Vern 1979

CHAPTER 30

Kathleen's Reflections

In thinking about my mother, Eleanor, and her story, things become clear:

> It takes all kinds to make this world go round,
> but it's the inventors who make it sound.
> Now I contend and some will agree,
> that it doesn't take a bird nest to fall far from the tree,
> before one wonders who was giving it the heave ho.
> So if it's the inventing bird you better watch out,
> for the big black bird who carries clout.
> One thing is clear, and it's plain to see,
> how really bad-mannered we humans can be.
> Inventors get ideas without strain,
> and these ideas become crystal clear as rain.
> But, when inventors get old, or are no longer needed,
> it's hard to get rid of what they seeded.
> Inventors have birthrights, with all of America at stake,
> but, their tickets are punched for a mad, mad take.
> Must the inventor forever claw and cower to keep from getting nailed?
> Must their lives and hearts forever be impaled?

KATHLEEN'S REFLECTIONS

The automobile title has maintained an unprecedented place, a part of acceptance in our world, but not the man who invented it. The Automobile Title Abstract was created and designed for the good of the people, no one would agree more. But because it produced revenue, and lots of it, it was ripe for the taking. It was only a matter of time before the greedy would rear their ugly heads.

Grandfather went to Washington on his eternal quest seeking justice, but wound up riding a nightmare into a world of harsh realities. He stood like a scarecrow in a lonely cornfield, shredded, tattered and torn, looking so forlorn, while the birds pecked at his straws one by one and carried them away to feather their own nests.

The story is not in vain for it is sadly true that some must suffer, or even die, in order for things to right themselves. We must be vigilant in learning these life lessons. This is why there is a need to reflect and remember.

So, if I were to ask a favor of any of you it would be, the next time you purchase a new car or obtain a title for an old one, that you pause for a moment and remember the true story of how the title system for the automobile came to be invented. **Cecil L. Snyder did exist**.

He was a philanthropist in his own right with his inventions, innovation and ideas. His legacy is acknowledged by his Christian descendants and is displayed in the billions of dollars the government reaps from the people in revenue every year, through automobile title registration.

Cecil had a great love for his country. This love is what drove him with his inspirational gifts to mankind. The government benefited greatly from his patented and copyrighted idea; yet not once has the government ever acknowledged him. As a descendant of Cecil L. Snyder, I believe he deserves recognition. This is why I pay tribute to my grandfather, may he rest in peace. There is no doubt in my mind; he truly was a fine gentleman, an uncommon man, an ***Inventor Anonymous***.

About the Author

I was born in the suburbs of Chicago, Illinois. I grew up in the area surrounding the O'Hare Airport in a small subdivision surrounded by cornfields. My mother, who was a dedicated wife, mother, and devout Christian woman, would lay the very foundation of Christian values now instilled in me. It is my faith in God that drives me to share this story about my grandfather and my mother's family. I've known about my grandfather's story since I was a young girl, from the many bits and pieces of information my mother shared with me about her life. It wasn't until I had a very vivid dream that I was compelled to reveal this story.

www.ingramcontent.com/pod-product-compliance
Lightning Source LLC
Chambersburg PA
CBHW071153070526
44584CB00019B/2773